I HOPE
IT'S NOT
HEREDITARY

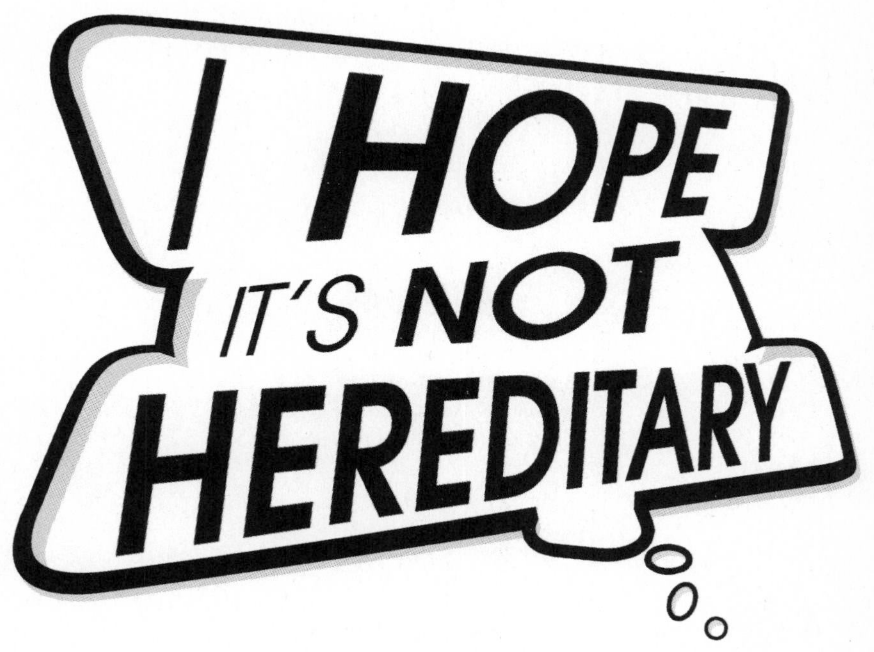

JEDIDIAH **HARTLEY**

WHITAKER HOUSE

I Hope It's Not Hereditary:
The mostly true stories of my father, Bob Hartley

Deeper Waters
310 W 106th St.
Kansas City, MO 64114

Mail to: P.O. Box 481007
Kansas City, MO 64114
1 (816) 765-9900
www.Bobhartley.org

ISBN: 978-1-62911-329-6
eBook ISBN: 978-1-62911-330-2
Printed in the United States of America

Whitaker House
1030 Hunt Valley Circle
New Kensington, PA 15068
www.whitakerhouse.com

Library of Congress Cataloging-in-Publication Data

Hartley, Jedidiah, 1991-
I hope it's not hereditary : the mostly true stories of my father, Bob Hartley / by Jedidiah Hartley with Bob Hartley.
pages cm
ISBN 978-1-62911-329-6 (trade pbk. : alk. paper) — ISBN 978-1-62911-330-2 (e-book)
1. Hartley, Bob, 1957- 2. Christian biography—United States. I. Title.
BR1725.H24155H37 2015
269'.2092—dc23
[B]

2015007474

1 2 3 4 5 6 7 8 9 10 11 ꟺ 22 21 20 19 18 17 16 15

TABLE OF CONTENTS

INTRODUCTION

There is a tendency for a child to define "normal" by the context of his surroundings. For instance, I grew up with three sisters and no brothers, so it wasn't until I was about sixteen that I realized tea parties, mud masks, and pretend weddings weren't a part of a young man's "normal" routine. And yet, occasionally, there are those things in life so far outside the ordinary that no matter how familiar you are with them, they are never normal and will never cease to surprise you. For me, this consistently unpredictable enigma has a name. Most call him Bob. I call him Dad.

Believe me when I say that there is no view of life where my dad fits remotely close into the context of normalcy. Maybe it is his voice, a voice so rough one would assume he eats thumb tacks for breakfast and gravel for lunch. Or maybe it is the way he would try to impress my friends by standing on his hands and drinking a glass of milk upside down. If that didn't work, then he would tackle them and put them in a sleeper hold until they admitted he was their favorite.

I've always admired my dad for his uniqueness. Sure, he was embarrassing, and sure, it was always hard to convince my friends to come over to my house, but he has always had a way of viewing and experiencing life that was refreshingly different. Although he has an extensive list of unconventional mannerisms, what sets him apart the most are his life stories. At twenty years old, my dad had collected twice as many stories as most people do in a lifetime. Even though I've heard his stories many times, they never cease to intrigue me.

And not just intrigue me, but also truly impact me. He endured a life full of pain and challenges—much of it self-induced, but some of it not—and yet he chose to hope, despite everything he'd been through. The countless stories he has collected are all testaments to his many hard-earned lessons. He has never swept his mistakes under the rug nor tried to blame them upon others. He embraced his mistakes, learned from them, and shared them openly with me, so I could build upon the hope he has fought for. His many stories were teaching me not to follow in his footsteps, but to stand on his shoulders.

And so this book is not meant to be read as a biographical account of Bob Hartley's life. While everything in this book is based upon the real memories of Bob Hartley, it may not be entirely factual. Some names, dates, events, and details have been changed. Some of the names of certain individuals have been changed as well for the sake of their own anonymity.

My purpose was never to be a historian. Rather, my only objective in writing this book has been to capture the heart of my father's incredible stories so that they might impact you in the same way they have impacted me.

An open letter to my dad:

Dear Pops,

Excitement. That was the main emotion we both shared when I first offered to write a book about your life. Now here we are, just a few weeks away from completing that book, and I think we share a new predominant emotion. It's the same emotion I get whenever I step up onto a stage and look out over a silent audience as they stare at me expectantly. It's the feeling I got just before debuting my first short film. Or even the feeling I got just before I played, for a girl I liked, a song I had written about her. I think the best word to describe that emotion would be *terror.*

I'm terrified because of how invested I am in the project. In a way, it is sort of my debut as an author, and I've really poured a considerable amount of time, effort, and soul into it. I want it to do well, but I really don't know how it will be received. Maybe I will get a great response (like that time I debuted my first short film). Or perhaps it will crash and burn in embarrassing failure (like that time I played the song for the girl I liked).

But as scary as it is for me, I can only imagine how terrifying it is for you.

When I first committed to write this book, I said my goal was to capture your story and, at the time, I didn't know what that really meant. I knew it would take a lot of hard work from both of us, but I had no idea how vulnerable it would require you to be.

You've shared with me everything you could remember about your upbringing: the good, the bad, and the ugly. And you've trusted me to take it all and put it into a book that we are sharing with the world.

That is terrifying. It's as if I painted a gigantic mural of you on the front of a billboard in Times Square. I've taken my understanding and viewpoint of all of your features, magnified them, and put them on display for anyone to see. And on top of all of that, I really haven't let you see that much of it. I wanted you to wait until it was complete so we could step back and look at the whole thing together.

Now here we are standing in Times Square looking at the almost-finished mural. We both are feeling more than a little bit vulnerable, because this isn't just a snapshot of your face, this a grand picture of your life.

It's not an impeccable depiction of reality, but that's what I think makes it honest. It is my best attempt to paint a picture that shows whom I see you to be: someone I look up to and admire greatly; someone who will never go down without a fight; someone who always has something to say and even more to do; someone who understands how flawed he is, yet also how loved he is. Someone with more compassion inside of him then he has ever has known what to do with, who is never afraid of a world that is already afraid, and who will never allow me to be anything less than who I was made to be.

And beyond all else, I see you as someone who will never, ever give up hope.

Your son,
Jed

1

I WOULD LIKE YOU TO MEET BOB HARTLEY

"What was it like growing up with your dad?" the young man in the snazzy business suit asked with such awe-struck wonder you would've thought I grew up with an extraterrestrial as a father. (That's not too far off, really.)

Does this guy have a name? I thought to myself as I stared at the young man, drawing a complete blank. It was the third day of a ministry conference that I had tagged along to with my dad, one of the main speakers at the event. My dad had asked me to come along with him to, in his words, "be a friend."

It was the fourth trip I had gone on with him in the last three months. A recent graduate, I had the time to give, and my dad didn't hesitate to take it. I wondered how I was going to make this look on my resume:

Friend of Bob Hartley (my dad) Sept.–Nov. 2013

- Helped facilitate and maintain my father's sanity as he traveled across the United States speaking at churches and conferences.
- Learned communication skills by often being randomly called upon in the middle of his sermons to tell some story, normally with as little direction as "tell them something funny and get them laughing—I'm tired."

The young man was still staring at me. Oh shoot, I never answered his question. I quickly fumbled for an answer.

"Yeah, it was great; he's a fun dad…." It was obvious by the guy's face that my answer was far from satisfactory. So I continued, "Well okay, how about I tell you a story?"

"Sure! Fire away!" the young man enthused.

He was hungry for information, that's for sure. I'm used to talking with people like him; my dad had a magnetic effect on people when he ministered. People want to find more out about him, his life, and his spiritual gifts, and if they can't get a meeting with him, they often come to me.

I don't mind it; in fact, I enjoy it. I like talking about my dad. I always tell the same story when people ask what it was like growing up with Bob Hartley, and here it is:

When I was fourteen years old I met a kid on my swim team named Andrew Butler. Andrew Butler was a cool kid. He had a social status beyond mine, good taste in music, a sense of style and, most importantly, he was a boy who had seemed to crack the code on how to talk to girls. I, on the other hand, was just nearing five feet tall, had a voice in the high soprano register, and wore braces. My interaction with girls had been, well, limited.

I admired Andrew for his suave personality and was eager to learn his ways. I had invited him over to my house to "you know, hang out, maybe watch a movie, and stuff." He had agreed and now we were finally bridging the gap between social acquaintances and friends.

I was in our family room giving Andrew a tour of our house when I first noticed my dad covertly approaching in the background. My heart sank. I had thought my dad was at work. I would have never brought Andrew over to my house if I had known my dad was there, at least not at this delicate stage in our friendship. Like a prowling lion, my dad crept towards Andrew. I shook my head at my dad in a futile attempt to dissuade him, but he had a look in his eyes that, most certainly, is the only accurate depiction of Survivor's "Eye of the Tiger." I had seen the look dozens of times before and knew trying to stop him would be like stepping in front of a two-hundred-car freight train.

With a sigh I turned to Andrew and apologized, then wished him good luck.

"Good luck with what?" Andrew asked, confused.

On cue Dad pounced from his hiding spot, and before Andrew had an opportunity to evaluate what was going on, Dad had him pinned to the ground and was threatening to pull out Andrew's nostril hairs if he didn't answer my dad's questions correctly: "Who are you and what are you doing in my house?" "How do you know Jed?" "Are you going to be a good influence on him?" "Do you love Jesus?" "Are you a Democrat?"

I, of course, knew this was my dad's own unique way of introducing himself; Andrew, of course, did not. I don't remember specifically what Andrew's answer was to any of these questions but I'm pretty sure it was something like:

"Aaaaaahhhhh!"

I tried to offer advice.

"Andrew, don't try to fight. Roll up into a ball, Andrew, roll up into a ball. Protect your vital organs."

And, like all of these spontaneous attacks, it ended with my dad suddenly releasing Andrew from a death grip, jumping up, and exclaiming: "I hope I just put the fear of God in you! Read your Bible more." And then he melted away.

I vividly remember Andrew's face at this point: a mixture of pure terror and intense perplexity. I could tell he was pondering what he should do about the events that had just unfolded: should he run straight out the front door and never look back, or call the police? But I didn't give him time to contemplate.

"Follow me!" I exclaimed as I raced out of the living-room.

"Where are we going?"

"Somewhere with a lock. He will be back," I hollered. And with that, Andrew collected himself and ran after me.

You know how you are taught in schools how to always be aware of the nearest exit in case of a fire? Well, growing up with the constant threat of a Bob attack, I quickly developed an instinctive awareness of which lockable room in our house was the closest at any given moment and how long it would take me to get there.

On the ground floor of our house, there was only one lockable door: the bathroom behind the kitchen, which happened to be on the other side of the house. I wasted no time and headed straight for it.

My mom had left earlier in the day, so Andrew and I were on our own. It was like *I Am Legend*. Andrew was Sam, I was Will Smith, and my dad the legion of athletic zombie/vampires. When the sun goes down (or my mom leaves the house) you really don't have any choice but to find someplace safe to hide and just hope they don't find you.

I quickly grabbed a handful of fruit snacks and several juice boxes in the pantry while we headed through the kitchen.

"What are you doing?" Andrew asked.

"Grabbing supplies…we might have to hunker down," I responded coolly.

"But your dad left, right?"

Again, as if on cue, Dad leapt from his hiding spot like a ninja—a loud, burley, Rocky Balboa-esque ninja. Andrew frantically tumbled into the bathroom as I followed closely behind, slamming the door and locking it behind me with practiced and perfected efficiency.

Now safe behind the locked door, I sighed a breath of relief.

"Your dad's crazy, man!" Andrew told me as he tried to calm himself. I nodded in agreement and then tossed Andrew a juice box.

It was a whole twenty minutes before Andrew finally brought up the conflict at hand. "Do you think it's safe? Your dad can't still be out there!"

"Oh, Andrew," I said with complete confidence. "He's still out there."

A quiet, but audible, snicker came from the other side of the door. If Andrew hadn't considered calling the police before, he absolutely did then. I haven't asked, but I believe that snicker frequents Andrew's nightmares still to this day.

Another twenty minutes and six juice boxes later, I realized that bunkering down in the bathroom had been a good idea as I now needed to utilize its available material resources. I walked around the corner to the toilet and lifted the lid. The bathroom is, and should always be, a place of security and solitude, and despite the impending danger that lurked just outside, I forced myself to relax. Then, all of the sudden, an explosion of ice cold water hit me directly in the face.

It was shocking, confusing, and terrifying all at the same time. At first I thought the toilet itself had exploded, but the constant stream was coming from my left, from the window.

Then I heard a deep, sinister laughter coming from outside. My dad had snuck out the door, grabbed the backyard garden hose, quietly cracked open the bathroom window, waited until I was in a vulnerable position, and then let loose, spraying gallons onto Andrew and I.

Well played, Dad, well played.

We had been outwitted, but this meant that Dad had left his post and the door was no longer guarded. Andrew and I bolted out of the bathroom and ran upstairs. I had read Sun Tzu's *The Art of War* so I knew that, when in battle, a warrior must always seek the higher ground. Plus, there were three rooms upstairs with lockable doors.

We rushed down the hall to our family's guest room. Possessing a solid door with a thick deadbolt lock, the guest room was, by far, the safest room in the whole house. We ran in, I shut the door and went to lock it—but then the unthinkable happened. The lock jammed. I panicked. The lock never jams. I heard my dad lumbering up the stairs: it was only moments before he got to us, and the door wouldn't lock! This was it. This was the end. He was going to catch us, gives us swirlies, and tickle us until we wet ourselves. Andrew had already endured so much; if Dad caught us for the third time, Andrew would certainly never come over again.

I had to think quickly. I threw the window open and jumped out onto the roof, and without a question Andrew followed me. I shut the window and ducked around the corner just as Dad lumbered into the guest room, only to discover it empty. Confused and defeated Dad began to retrace his steps.

Andrew and I viewed the neighborhood as we sat proudly perched atop the roof. It was late in the evening of a clear summer day and as I watched the sun set, I smiled with such a sense of accomplishment, you would've thought I had just climbed Mt. Everest. I had seen this view a hundred times before, but something about evading near death just makes everything that much more beautiful.

And then, for the second time in one day, I was hit in the face with an unexpected stream of water while Dad roared with maniacal laughter. I nearly tumbled off of the roof in shock. We were two stories up, how the heck did he reach us with the garden hose? I followed the stream of water to see that my dad had drug the garden hose inside, up the stairs, through the bedroom, and out the window. I marveled at his dedication.

There was nothing we could do; he had blocked our only exit. I turned and shielded my face from the onslaught of water as I accepted our crushing defeat. But then, at the end of the road, I saw a silver Dodge Caravan make a left onto our street. For a second I froze.

"DAD, STOP! Mom's here!"

Dad dropped the garden hose. This had just gotten real. Any look of fear that had come across Andrew's face earlier in the day paled in comparison to the look of pure horror that my dad now wore. However, the look quickly changed to one of determination and, in an instant, my dad was back inside the house and heading down the stairs. Aware that this was a matter of life and death for my dad, I jumped to my father's aid—literally. There was a grassy patch on the side of the house that I flung myself at. I hit the ground, did a quick tuck and roll, zipped over to the garden hose, and turned the faucet off.

My dad crashed out of the back door. Again, I'm speaking literally. He was in such a hurry that he didn't bother using the door handle. He just put his shoulder down and busted out. Luckily the door was slightly ajar so he didn't have to rip it off its hinges—although, believe me, he could have and he would have. With lightening hand-over-hand speed, he pulled the hose out from within the house and tossed it into a jumbled mess outside the backdoor.

We both rushed back inside to see that Andrew had already grabbed a beach towel and mopped up the bathroom floor. Andrew had no idea what my mom would do if she discovered what my dad had been up too, but he understood enough to know he didn't want to find out firsthand. Dad grabbed the wet towel from Andrew and tossed it into the garbage can: there couldn't be any evidence. But Andrew and I both were still soaking wet. Thinking fast, Dad led us both into the kitchen.

As my mom opened the front door and walked into the kitchen, Dad stuck my head underneath the kitchen faucet.

"In the name of the Father, the Son, and the Holy Spirit," he said as he turned on the water and let it wash over my face.

"What is going on?" my mom asked inquisitively. She had been married to my dad for over twenty years now and could sniff out mischief from a mile away.

"Oh honey, you're home!" Dad said with a cheery smile. "The boys, they asked if they could be baptized! Isn't that great?"

My mom eyed Dad suspiciously and then looked to Andrew. "Is that so?"

Andrew smiled, "Hallelujah, thank you Jesus." The kid was catching on.

"Well, you're getting my kitchen all wet," my mom said with a sigh.

I then perked up, "Yeah; we thought of that. Dad just told me we would put a pool in the backyard to make it easier for future baptismal ceremonies." I had been trying to convince my dad to shell out for a pool for a long time. Dad smiled and nodded. He was in a dangerous position, and we both knew he had to agree with me. We never ended up getting a pool, but hey, it was worth a shot.

"Hmm, well, you better think of something, because there will be no more getting water in my kitchen. Bob, take these boys out back and dry them off."

"Yeah, you bet honey, in fact I was just about to take them out for ice cream. Come on boys, let's get you out of the house."

—— – – ——

I've seen Bob Hartley minister in hundreds of different churches to thousands of individuals. I've heard him called a prophet in charismatic settings, an oracle by a bishop in a Catholic church, and some not very nice things by a few rather uptight individuals in certain Norwegian Baptist circles. But when I hear the name Bob Hartley, I think of the man who dragged the garden hose up through our house and onto our roof so he could spray me and my friend with water. That's the man that I grew up with.

2

IGNORANT EXPERIENCE

"When I was a boy of fourteen, my father was so ignorant I could hardly stand to have the old man around. But when I got to be twenty-one, I was astonished at how much the old man had learned in seven years."
—attributed to Mark Twain

My dad and I grew up very different people in very different worlds. Even in physical appearance, we couldn't be more opposite. Take the physique of Sylvester Stallone, the height of Tom Cruise, the eyebrows of Einstein, and the once-chiseled but now slightly padded gut of Dog the Bounty Hunter, throw them all together and you've got Bob Hartley. I, on the other hand, possess the height and frame of a Kenyan marathon runner, the curly afro of *That '70s Show*'s Steven Hyde, and the muscle content of Ichabod Crane.

Growing up, my favorite sports were soccer and swimming. Dad grew up as a wrestler.

"Dance around and kick the ball! Ooh, someone touched you—fall over and start crying," Dad would mock whenever I attempted to explain the value of soccer.

"At least I'm not prancing around with other men dressed in leotards!" I would retort.

While I have always valued art, he has always valued business. Neither of us understands a lick about the other.

"Hey Dad, listen to this song I wrote," I would say, as I showed him my latest piano composition.

"Oh, cool! How are we going to make money off of it? Can you record it and sell it? Here, I will help you; let me call a hundred different music producers I have met and tell them you want to record and sell an album," Dad would say supportively, but completely missing the substance of musical expression.

When watching movies, I like to immerse myself into the story, shutting out everything else so I can focus on the film. This, of course, never works well when watching films with my dad. He wants to stop the movie every ten minutes to get up and use the restroom, run to the grocery store to get low-fat ice cream, ask what is going on in the film, or demand to know how it ends.

And speaking of which, he is physically incapable of handling tragic endings. After high school, I went to film school where I wrote several short films. In one, the main character dies at the end of the film. When I showed the final film to my dad, he had a hard time understanding why I would "kill" his favorite character.

"Wait, Greg died?" my dad asked, dumbfounded as the credits rolled.

"Yeah, it was the sacrifice he had to make in order to save his friends," I tried to explain.

"So you killed Greg?" he asked, still in shock.

"Well, I didn't *really* kill him, but, yes, he died."

"Hmm...," Dad pondered for a few moments. Then he looked up at me with distinct concern on his face. "How is your relationship with the Lord, Jed? Are you getting a good amount of devotional time in?"

In fact, as I grew up, the only unflinching similarity we both possessed was a devotion to the Kansas City Chiefs football team (and a mutual sense of heartbreak and disappointment at their lack of success throughout the years). But beyond that, there are not many personality traits, interests, or hobbies we share.

Because of these differences, my dad and I had a convoluted mixture of mutual admiration peppered with an unfortunate amount of disregard throughout my teenage years. As much as I really liked my dad and enjoyed spending time with him, he seemed so detached from my own reality.

Especially because his own life seemed so eventful. When I was young I took everything my dad said as gospel truth.

"Yep, that's when I had to wrestle Boris the Russian heavyweight champ to end the Cold War," my dad would say, beginning his account of a historical match with a gargantuan, Russian brute that the two hostile nations had bet their entire futures upon. "I pinned him within the first round, saving the world from nuclear fallout!" he told me, as I listened with wide eyes and a dropped jaw.

It's got to be true, I would think to myself. I mean, how couldn't it be? The stories were so exciting, and he told them with such passion and detail, I just couldn't help but believe them.

Eventually, I grew up and realized that my dad had never actually saved the world by winning a wrestling match. He just made up the whole story. The older I got, the more his great yarns began to unravel. Turns out, he was neither an astronaut nor a CIA spy, and most disappointingly, he was never the fifth member of The Beatles. Thus began my lifelong battle of separating Bob Hartley, the man, from Bob Hartley, the myth.

One day in my early teenage years, my dad decided to take me on a tour around Kansas City to show me all of the homes and neighborhoods in which he had lived while growing up. When we arrived at the first neighborhood, he pointed out a home with a broken stoop.

"You see that? That stoop was broken by an elephant stepping on it!" he said with a nostalgic smile.

We then turned and headed down a different street.

"Here is where Mike O'Hara saved my life," he said, pointing to a large hill with a fence at the bottom.

He then drove about three minutes down the road and stopped again.

"And here is where your Uncle Jimmy saved my life—well, the first time he saved my life, anyway."

Dad never took enough time to fully explain these stories, because he would always get distracted by something he saw and then he would start in on another story. "Oh, and here is where I was in the middle of a gang shootout—"

Have you ever watched an episodic TV show or read a novel series and stopped to wonder how it is that the hero of the story always seems to find himself in the most unusual and fantastical of situations? That is the feeling I was beginning to get while driving with my dad.

"There's no way you were in a shootout!" I said, indignantly.

My dad then went on to explain how he was working as a manager for the Ramada Inn at the time. Often he and one of his coworkers would carpool to work. One day, while dropping off the coworker at his house after a full night shift, someone drove by and started shooting at them. The coworker was a part of a gang, and the drive-by shooter was a rival gang member who had spent all night staking out the coworker's house. My dad told me his unbelievable story as I listened, skeptically.

"I'm telling you, Jed, as soon as he stepped out of the car, BAM! BAM! BAM! Bullets started whizzing by! My coworker immediately dropped to the ground, pulled a gun out of his jacket, and began to return fire while using my van as cover! I leaned over under the gun fire and rolled down the window. 'Hey, I think I'm going to head out now,' I yelled to my coworker as I kept my head as low as possible. My coworker stood up and stuck his head in my open window. 'Oh yeah, see you later. Thanks for the ride.' I nodded, backed up my car, and headed home."

I was convinced my dad was making up all of these stories as we went along. I was not a little kid anymore, and I knew things like this just didn't happen. Or at least so I thought.

They say truth is stranger than fiction. Well, that phrase has never been more applicable than when referring to Bob Hartley. Every once in a while, when visiting with my extended family, they will bring up one of the stories I thought my dad had fabricated. They will reminisce about the many times my uncle saved my dad's life, the shootout, or even when one of their neighbors owned a pet baby elephant that broke their stoop.

"Wait, that actually happened?" I would ask.

"Oh yeah, of course," they would confirm.

My dad would shoot me a look, as if to say, "See? I told you so!" I would just shake my head, completely flabbergasted.

How does my dad always happen to find himself in such extraordinary circumstances? I would think.

I've realized that he does not just "happen" to find himself in the midst of incredible circumstances; he creates them. The combination of his wit, outspoken demeanor, ambitious attitude, and complete lack of concern for other people's perception of him all come together to create a perfect story storm. And that storm constantly follows him, leaving a wake of tall tales wherever he goes.

But although he told me disjointed stories, I knew precious little of his personal, internal journey. Burned by his tall tales, I was dismissive of his words of correction, too. I felt misunderstood by a dad whose life experience was so foreign to my own. He would share conclusions he had formed through years and years of experience but, because I knew little of the backstory, I would sweep them under the rug until I later learned what had prompted the conclusion, or, better yet, saw their applications come to life firsthand.

It's like when my friend Kerry first taught me how to drive a motorcycle. He explained how to push the handle bar in the opposite direction of the way you want to go when making turns at high speeds. Logically, you would think pointing your front wheel to the left would make you go left, but if you go try it, you'll find yourself veering right. Don't ask me why, because to this day, I have no idea how it works. Go ask a physics professor or something. Kerry had no idea why either, but he had been riding motorcycles all his life, so, of course, I listened to him. I could've argued with Kerry about how it didn't make logical sense, and I might have even won the argument. But at the end of the day, I would have still wound up crashing if I didn't heed his advice.

The same goes for my dad. He would share truths with me that he had discovered, some that had good logic behind them, but some like Kerry's knowledge of driving a motorcycle—at first take, they sound ridiculous.

"No, that doesn't make sense," I would say. "It doesn't work that way."

"Just trust me," Dad would respond. "I know what I'm talking about."

I regret not trusting him more. Like many young men my age, I regret not listening more. I regret not knowing sooner his personal story, his incredible experiences. I do believe I could have avoided some serious crashes.

3

BULLDOG BOB

Robert Hartley, or Bobby, as he was often called by his family, was born to John and Ann Hartley on August 12, 1957, in Menorah Medical Center, a frantic twenty-minute drive from their home in Raytown, Missouri. Just a month after Bobby's first birthday, a tornado ripped through their town, destroying several homes and buildings. It hit Ruskin, a local high school, demolishing most of the facility, even tearing the "s" and "k" off of the school sign, leaving it to read "RU-IN High School". The Hartleys were living in a little one-story ranch house at the time. Just before the tornado hit, Ann and John had to rush their family to a neighbor's house for shelter.

After the tornado, John promptly moved his family to a new house in Saint Catherine's Gardens, where the family lived for the next fifteen years. The Hartleys, a big family with rambunctious children possessing large social appetites, fit well inside the Saint Catherine's Gardens neighborhood. Saint Catherine's was full of big Catholic families crawling with young kids. Bobby grew up with something fun to do at every moment and plenty of opportunities to get into trouble. He was a stocky little boy, gifted with an insatiable hunger for mischief and adventure. Early in middle school, Bobby was appropriately nicknamed "Bulldog Bob" by his peers. The nickname fit him well. He was small but tough, and what he lacked in size he made up for in pure aggression. He would pick fights with kids who severely outmatched him, and as much as his father and mother tried to train him, his domestication was a lost hope.

Saint Catherine's Gardens was so full of large families, several busses were required to collect the sheer volume of children on Bobby's street for school. He always enjoyed the bus rides, partly because he was a social butterfly and cramming that many of his friends onto one bus was a dream come true, but chiefly because of Billy. Billy was the neighborhood kid who collected rotten bananas and threw them at the bus as it drove by. Bobby never quite figured out how Billy was able to amass such a large quantity of bananas, but somehow he did. Without fail, he would attack the bus every morning with an onslaught of sloppy mush. He never got caught because he strategically varied his point of attack, never hiding in one place too often and always having an open escape route. However, Billy probably didn't even need such a level of strategic ingenuity. The bus lady was a short, hefty lump of a woman, who, despite her best efforts, could never waddle fast enough to catch him.

The bus ride was about the only aspect of school that Bobby actually enjoyed. His school was tightly structured and emphasized the use of firm discipline. Many of the teachers maintained a strict set of rules in the classroom and took pride in being feared by the students. The most feared of all the teachers was Mr. Freed. Just the mention of his name sent chills down the spines of even the toughest students. The embodiment of the no-nonsense Catholic church he attended on Sundays, Mr. Freed stood six feet three inches tall with a thin, wiry frame, the religiously well-tamed haircut and shaven face of a drill sergeant, and the wild, untamed eyebrows of a mad scientist. With a piercing stare, an unflinching moral code, and a petrifying Machiavellian demeanor, Mr. Freed ruled his classroom all too effectively.

At lunch, students would murmur in hushed tones horror stories about the dreaded Mr. Freed.

"I heard a couple years back he got a kid expelled for just giving him a funny look," one student shared.

Another chimed in, "I heard that he gives swats so bad, you can't sit down for a month!"

It was a day and age when the punishment for misbehavior was direct, and no one was more direct than Mr. Freed. If you misbehaved in his class, rather than notifying your parents, Mr. Freed dished out punishment himself. An avid golfer and three-time college arm wrestling champion, Mr. Freed's swats had reached a level of infamy among the students. No one dared cross him, for no student was gutsy or foolish enough to do so. No one, that is, except for Bobby Hartley.

It was three weeks into Bobby's sixth grade year when he first got the idea to tie Mr. Freed's shoelaces to the desk. You see, each Friday, Mr. Freed would end class with snippets of educational films. Robotic in more ways than one, Mr. Freed would systematically pull the projector out, start the reel, sit back in his chair, kick up his legs onto the desk, and fall asleep. Like clockwork, Mr. Freed would wake up just as the reel was winding down and then dismiss the class. It was a bold and vulnerable move to fall asleep among a class of ornery preteens, but similar to a bear during hibernation, Mr. Freed slept without any touch of trepidation, knowing no one would dare wake him.

Bobby figured he could silently sneak up on Mr. Freed while he was asleep and tie his shoelaces to the desk, then crawl back to his chair and, when Mr. Freed woke up, enjoy the spectacle of his whole class laughing at their mighty and terrifying teacher struggling to get to his feet. There was no thought of repercussions or any extrapolation of possible negative outcomes in Bobby's mind. His thought process began and ended with the temptation of besting Mr. Freed.

Bobby dispatched rumors of his audacious scheme among his friends and fellow students. Anticipation swelled and, each Friday, a greater number of his classmates would fixate their attention on Bobby as Mr. Freed fell asleep. Several Fridays came and went, and Bobby still had not accomplished his daring feat. Some students speculated that he had lost his nerve. But, cool as a cucumber, Bobby was too dumb to be afraid. Instead, an intuitive entertainer, he knew that each week he waited, he only increased the class's anticipation.

By the fifth Friday, the tension had reached a pinnacle. Bobby listened to the constant whir of the projector, mixed in with the rumble of Mr. Freed's snoring. Bobby leaned over and whispered to his best friend, Mike O'Hara, "It's time. I'm going to do it."

O'Hara, a couple of years wiser than Bobby, shook his head and tried to talk some sense into his foolish friend.

"No, don't. You'll regret it!"

But it was too late; Bobby had already dropped to his knees beneath his desk and begun to scurry toward his target. As Bobby inched closer, beads of sweat began to percolate his brow and slide down his face. The class brimmed with suspense as Bobby slowly rose up and began to untie Mr. Freed's shoelaces. He imagined Mr. Freed struggling with his laces while the whole class broke into hysterical laughter. He suppressed a snicker as he draped the loose laces over the front bar of the desk and tied them into the best sailor's knot he could manage. As he dropped back to the ground and army crawled to his desk, the class was silent. He could sense the silent ovation that emanated from his awestruck peers. He slid up in his chair and gave a nod to O'Hara, which basically said, "Yeah, aren't you glad you know me?"

O'Hara glanced toward Mr. Freed, then back at Bobby. "Bobby, what if he falls over? He could really get hurt!"

Bobby hadn't considered that Mr. Freed could actually topple over, and the notion certainly gave him pause. But he quickly shrugged it off, dismissing O'Hara's fears.

But O'Hara continued. "He is going to know it was you! The whole class saw you do it; someone is bound to tell."

Bobby hadn't thought of this. Panic enveloped him, as he began to take into account the consequences of his actions. Of course someone would tell on him. Mr. Freed could make a kid crack without even looking at him. Bobby glanced at the projector; the reel of film was getting dangerously low, but there was still time. Bobby dropped to his knees and scurried back towards Mr. Freed's desk.

"What are you doing?" O'Hara questioned.

"I have to untie them! If he finds out it was me, I'm dead!" Bobby responded.

Bobby reached Mr. Freed's desk, grabbed the laces, and, with far less stealth and composure than before, began to untie the shoelaces. He struggled with the knot, cursing himself for how tight he tied it. He hadn't noticed it before, but Bobby began to realize that Mr. Freed's snoring sounded much more like growling then actual snoring.

In desperation, Bobby yanked at the knot, when, all of the sudden, the reel of film began to click. The film was moments away from finishing. Mr. Freed stirred and dropped his feet beneath the desk. Bobby looked in horror at Mr. Freed's dangling feet. Once again, he tried to pull at the knot, but it was no use. When Mr. Freed dropped his feet, the knots had pulled taut. Bobby looked desperately around the classroom.

"Someone give me scissors!" he whispered.

Dozens of students ripped open their desk and rifled through their stuff looking for scissors. But it was too late. Mr. Freed lifted his hands and began to rub his eyes; he was waking up. For the fourth and final time, Bobby dropped to the ground and began to crawl away. He made it halfway back to his desk when, all of the sudden, he heard a crash.

Boom!

Mr. Freed fell over his desk and collapsed in a heap onto the floor. Papers flew across the room. Contrary to the way he had originally imagined it, there were no peals of laughter from the class, only stunned, terrified silence. Bobby slowly looked over his shoulder at Mr. Freed to assess the damage.

The teacher lay on his side with his head propped up on his arm, staring straight at Bobby. "Mr. Hartley," Mr. Freed said coolly.

"I'm just looking for my pencil, Mr. Freed, just looking for my pencil," Bobby desperately tried to explain.

"Swats!" The word struck Bobby like a judge's gavel. The bell rang and Bobby bolted out the door, across the road, and kept running, all the way home.

That was the longest weekend of Bobby's life. Saturday morning, he dragged himself out of bed only to collapse on the floor in a heap, burdened by the immeasurable weight of his dread and self-pity.

In actuality, his current state stemmed more from his overly melodramatic personality than his actual fear of ensuing punishment. Undoubtedly, Bobby was more affected by his failure than by his punishment. He had set out to best Mr. Freed and he had failed, miserably. Instead of inspiring awe among his classmates, he had only evoked pity.

After an hour of wallowing, Bobby eventually pulled out his journal. If this were to be his last couple of days on earth, there were a few things he needed to address. He began to scribble down his last will and testament. This didn't take very long considering he was twelve and the only real possession he had was a stack of *Mad* magazines.

It was shaping up to be a dark day for Bobby, and it would have remained that way if it weren't for O'Hara. Knowing his friend would be in need of a good distraction, O'Hara showed up at Bobby's front door that morning and invited him to the local high school football game. Bobby was hesitant at first, but he reluctantly agreed. During the game, O'Hara did his best to dig Bobby out of his dismal mood.

"How about a hot dog? I brought mayonnaise!" O'Hara said, as he pulled a handful of Miracle Whip packets from out of his coat pocket.

Normally these were the guaranteed ingredients to cheer up Bobby, but even a greasy hot dog with an excess of packaged mayo was not enough to change his mood. Still, it wasn't like he was going to pass up a free hot dog. Bobby forced his best smile and nodded to O'Hara in approval. As O'Hara left for the school's concession stand, Bobby noticed Steve Vanhooky sitting on the other side of the bleachers.

Vanhooky, who lived a couple of blocks over, was the biggest, meanest kid Bobby had ever met. With his black leather jacket, hair slicked back with a pound of Crisco, and a pack of cigarettes rolled up in his sleeve, Steve knew all about being tough. Normally Bobby would head in the opposite direction whenever he saw Vanhooky. The kid walked around with something to prove and would leap at the slightest opportunity for a fight. But stupidity has a greedy appetite. The more you feed it, the hungrier it gets, and Bobby had been slipping his stupidity extra portions for far too long. Maybe it was because he was feeling the need to prove himself after the previous day's failure, or perhaps because obnoxiousness was the only way he could cheer himself up. But, for whatever reason, Bobby snuck up behind Vanhooky and prepared to pounce.

With a couple of hot dogs in his hand, O'Hara turned the corner and paused, perplexed, when he saw Bobby crouching behind the meanest kid in the city. What was Bobby planning?

"HEY, VANHOOKY!" Bobby screamed at the top of his lungs. Vanhooky, shocked, dropped the cigarette he had just lit. Then, with all of the might his twelve-year-old body could muster, Bobby slapped his hands on Vanhooky's ears. Bobby scampered down the bleachers, roaring with laughter as Vanhooky toppled off his seat in pain. It took a couple of seconds for Vanhooky to recover, but when he did, he bolted up and tore after Bobby with a vengeful ferocity.

Without a moment's hesitation, Bobby leapt over the guardrail and onto the field—in the middle of the football game. He weaved through the players and across the field. Hot on his tail, Vanhooky barreled his way through the team, tossing kids aside like pillows. Bobby cleared the visitor's bench and darted across the parking lot. Due to a surge of pure adrenaline, Bobby separated himself from the raging Vanhooky.

Bobby kept running and made it all the way back to his house without breaking stride. Elated and with a newfound sense of courage, he forgot all about Mr. Freed and his impending swats. Later that afternoon, Bobby met up with O'Hara. Over a pack of hot dogs and a fair helping of mayonnaise, the two talked of how Bobby's courage would be legendary for centuries to come.

The next day Bobby went to Mass as he did every Sunday morning to appease his father who insisted it was good for a young boy. He found it hard to stay awake that early in the morning, and even harder to pay attention. The routine was the same as always. Mass began with a few cold and empty hymns from sometime during the Middle Ages that gave you as many chills as the castles in which they were composed. The priest of the church then shared principles of dedication and self-discipline while a horde of nuns, who possessed a sense of right and wrong as black and white as the dresses they wore, swept the congregation with eyes peeled for the slightest wrong committed by the children in attendance.

It was too much for Bobby; he didn't care for any of it, and from what he could tell, it didn't care much for him. So he would duck away and hide himself in a small cubbyhole he had discovered in the back of the church. Tucked inside a narrow corridor created between two outer walls of the church, the cubbyhole was small, damp, and dark, but it beat going to Mass. Each week, Bobby would wait there until the service finished, then he would grab a church bulletin before he left, so if his father ever asked him how it went, Bobby could just hand him the bulletin and say, "Here, see for yourself."

Bobby stocked the cubbyhole with necessary supplies: a yo-yo he nabbed from his older brother, a stack of *Mad* magazines, a box of Twinkies, and a green spiral notebook his father had given to him as a prayer journal. But as Bobby arrived at Mass this particular Sunday morning, he actually considered attending the service. He figured it might benefit him to get on God's good side before facing Mr. Freed the next day. Maybe if he got right with God, "the Big Man" would come to his aid. Maybe He would send a tornado or an earthquake, a swarm of locusts, the rapture—anything that would cancel school and save him from the wrath of Mr. Freed. But Bobby quickly dismissed the idea, because from what he knew, God was just as strict as Mr. Freed. It would take more than a morning of repentance to make up for Bobby's history of mischief. So, as he did every Sunday, Bobby snuck away to his cubbyhole and spent the time reading his magazines.

Monday morning came upon Bobby quicker than he thought possible. The adrenaline from his run-in with Vanhooky had worn off, and the familiar weight of dread hung on his shoulders. But as Bobby was getting ready, he suddenly had an idea. He tore open his drawers, pulled out every pair of underwear he owned, and put them on. He didn't stop there, either. He then went to the garage, ripped up a couple of boxes, and stuffed them between pairs of underwear. His jeans were now too small to fit around his heavily padded bottom, so Bobby ran into his older brother's room and stole a pair of his jeans. When he slid them on, they fit perfectly. *This might just work!* He thought.

Bobby had to waddle around school the whole day leading up to Mr. Freed's class, but he figured it was well worth the trouble. Finally, Mr. Freed's class period arrived, and Bobby scooted into class, half sitting, half standing at his desk as the teacher walked in. Mr. Freed locked eyes with Bobby and nodded: it was time to face the music. Without a word, he followed Mr. Freed into a side room. Bobby leaned over and Mr. Freed, switch in hand, cocked back his arm and prepared to strike. Bobby gritted his teeth and prepared for impact.

SLAP!

Bobby heard the crack of the switch, but, to his great joy, he didn't feel a thing! The eight pairs of underwear and six layers of cardboard had done their job. Not wanting Mr. Freed to know his punishment was ineffective, Bobby let out his best and most convincing yelp. Mr. Freed raised his hand and swung again. Again, Bobby heard the slap of the switch but felt nothing.

"Oh, Mr. Freed, please have mercy!" Bobby whimpered, impressed at his own acting abilities. Mr. Freed continued to dish out a heavy dose of punishment as Bobby continued to feign pain, even going so far as to muster up tears. After a considerable amount of swats, Mr. Freed let up.

"All right, Bobby, you can head back to class," Mr. Freed said, with an uncharacteristic hint of compassion.

"Okay. I'm really sorry, Mr. Freed," Bobby said, with a convincing but entirely inauthentic sniffle. Still whimpering, Bobby limped back into the classroom, as Mr. Freed stayed back for a moment to return his switch to its proper place.

"Bobby, are you okay?" O'Hara asked empathetically.

Bobby cracked a grin. "Ah, he hits like a girl."

The whole class was silent and in awe. O'Hara needed an explanation. "But...how?"

"I'm wearing an entire drawer of underwear!" Bobby had been whispering at first to keep Mr. Freed from hearing him in the other room, but as he continued to brag he slowly lost control of his volume. "He thought I was hurting. I didn't feel a darn thing. I told you I could—"

He stopped mid-sentence as a sudden change in the visage of the class alerted him. Their expressions of elation and awe had melted into looks of horror. Bobby felt a cold chill run across his back.

Slowly, Bobby turned and looked over his shoulder, meeting the eyes of Mr. Freed who was now standing in the doorway just behind him, arms crossed, a scowl on his face. Bobby stammered, trying to come up with an excuse.

"Save it, Hartley," Mr. Freed said. "Swats again tomorrow!"

Bobby dropped his head in defeat.

4

FACING CONSEQUENCES

Bobby kicked a couple of rocks as he slowly meandered home. As he turned down his street, he saw O'Hara, a wet sponge in hand and a dry towel draped over his shoulder, washing his parents' car in their driveway.

"Why is it that I do the things I do?" Bobby asked.

O'Hara smiled and dropped his sponge into a bucket of soapy water.

"All I would've had to do was keep my mouth shut and I would've been home free," Bobby continued. "But no, I had to go and brag to the entire class—"

Bobby would have continued, but O'Hara had stopped paying attention and was looking past Bobby down the street.

"What? What is it?" Bobby asked. Then he turned and saw for himself.

Steve Vanhooky was walking up the street with three of his buddies, and they were headed straight for Bobby. For a moment, Bobby considered running away, but he still had on eight pairs of underwear and oversized jeans; running away wasn't going to be all that easy. He kept his head down and avoided making eye contact as Vanhooky and his three friends walked up the driveway.

Although Bobby wasn't looking at him, he could feel the anger and hatred coming from Vanhooky as he came closer and closer. Vanhooky didn't say a thing; he didn't need to—he had been humiliated by Bobby, and now it was payback time. But just as Vanhooky got to Bobby, O'Hara stepped between them.

"Leave him alone," O'Hara said, as he stood toe to toe with Vanhooky. O'Hara was a tough kid himself, a couple years older and a lot bigger than Bobby. Still, he was no match for Vanhooky, much less Vanhooky and his gang.

"He's a little kid; he wasn't thinking; give him a break," O'Hara continued, trying his best to diffuse the situation, but it was a trivial attempt. Vanhooky's anger was not assuaged through discussion.

"Out of my way, O'Hara, or it'll be you instead of him," Vanhooky said, without an ounce of compassion.

"Okay," O'Hara said, with a shrug. "Then it'll be me."

Bobby could hardly believe his friends answer. *Would he really take the beating for me?* Bobby thought to himself. Within a split second, he had his answer.

Vanhooky threw an uppercut into O'Hara's jaw which sent him flying back into his parents' car. Quickly, Vanhooky's friends grabbed O'Hara and held him up, as Vanhooky buried punch after punch into the boy's ribs.

Bobby stepped back in shock. He could hardly compose himself as he watched his best friend get pummeled on his behalf. O'Hara doubled over in pain and Vanhooky's buddies let him crumble to the ground. Blood gushed out of his nose and he gasped for air. Vanhooky's punches had completely knocked the wind out of O'Hara.

For a second, Bobby thought it was over, but then Vanhooky grabbed O'Hara, slid him over to the soap bucket, and shoved his head inside, holding him submerged in the soapy water. O'Hara flailed desperately, trying to get his head out of the water, as Bobby looked on, horrified.

Unable to stand and watch anymore, Bobby shouted, "Stop it!" As he ran towards Vanhooky, one of Vanhooky's friends grabbed him by the shirt tail. Bobby twisted back and slugged the boy in the stomach as hard as he could. The boy doubled over in pain and released Bobby. Now free, he flung himself at Vanhooky in a desperate attempt to help O'Hara, whose head was still submerged in the soapy bucket. But Vanhooky let go of O'Hara and turned to forcefully shove Bobby back, sending him hurtling to the ground in a heap as O'Hara pulled his head out of the bucket and gasped for air. As the two lay on the ground, O'Hara coughing up water and desperately trying to regain his breath and Bobby looking up terrified, Vanhooky calmly pulled out a cigarette and lit it. Then, after several puffs, Vanhooky walked off, satisfied.

Bobby immediately scrambled over to O'Hara and helped him to his feet.

"Why?" Bobby asked, struggling to find the right words. "Why would you do something like that for me?"

O'Hara looked at Bobby's confused and grateful face. "You are my best friend," he said. "Of course I'd fight for you."

——— - - ———

The next day and the following week seemed to drift by for Bobby. The swats he received from Mr. Freed the next day were painful, but not nearly as painful as watching his best friend take a beating on his behalf. Neither boy ever brought up what happened.

For O'Hara, it was not a big deal. He walked around with a black eye and a fat lip for a week or so, but otherwise, life went on like normal. For Bobby, however, it was monumental. He couldn't understand why anyone would care enough to take such punishment for him. Bobby never asked for O'Hara's protection, nor did he ever expect for O'Hara to suffer on his behalf.

The following Sunday, Bobby once again went to Mass, only to slip away and hide in his cubbyhole. The events of the week rolled around in his head and weighed on his soul. Thinking of what O'Hara had done brought a guilt to the pit of his gut. Had he known that O'Hara would've been the one to take the beating, Bobby would have never messed with Vanhooky in the first place.

Bobby never thought much about the consequences of his actions. He was a boy who lived in the moment and saw personal risk as more enticing than frightening. *Big deal if I get in trouble,* Bobby would think.

But as he sat in his cubbyhole, with the faint preaching of the Catholic priest ringing in the background, Bobby began to realize how his actions had brought so much pain to his friend. Given the choice, Bobby would have rather received the temporary physical pain of swats, or even a beating from Vanhooky, rather than the lingering pain from the guilt of inflicting suffering upon his best friend. Yet, as guilty as Bobby felt, he was also comforted by the thought that someone cared enough to endure pain on his behalf. It warmed his heart to know that he had such a good friend.

Unsure how to process what had happened, and not really wanting to think about it anymore, he began to read his *Mad* magazine. But he was unable to focus, and before long gave up and put the magazine down. The priest's voice was muffled by the thick walls so that Bobby couldn't make out what he was saying.

He's probably saying something mean, Bobby thought. The Father wore a permanent scowl and Bobby always wondered why the man was always so angry. Regardless, Bobby was just glad not to be in the service. He really didn't want to have to endure a stale and intimidating lecture from a discontent, self-righteous man—lectures that seemed meant to only inform Bobby how angry and disappointed God was with him.

Bobby mused upon the story he had heard, over and over again, while growing up in his Catholic household—how God had come to earth as a man named Jesus and had died for humanity. Bobby never quite understood the story, specifically why Jesus had to die. Bobby began to wonder if that was why God was always so mad; He came down and died so the world would be better, but people like Bobby kept screwing up and breaking rules, making His death pointless.

He hated to think about how much God must hate him. So he decided he was going to pretend that God *didn't* hate him. He began to pretend God wasn't actually a strict, angry disciplinarian like Mr. Freed; he pretended God was actually a friend—a friend like O'Hara—someone who cared enough to suffer on Bobby's behalf.

Bobby reached beneath his stack of magazines and pulled out his little green journal. He had never actually written anything in it, but had just kept it around for appearances' sake. He certainly had never written a prayer and really didn't know what to say. But he pretended that God wouldn't care if he failed to say the right thing. So he wrote,

> I don't understand why you had to die;
> It makes me want cry.
> Would you please hold on real tight?
> I believe there is going to be a fight.

Bobby scribbled the words into his journal. It felt good to pretend that God cared about him.

5

JOHN HARTLEY'S SENSE OF HOPE

When I was the same age as Bobby scribbling during mass, I wasn't trouncing bullies: I was making up stories. One favorite—and perhaps the craziest—was about my grandfather, John Hartley, or *Umpa,* as his grandchildren called him, and his full head of wispy white hair.

I used to stare at my grandfather's hair, fascinated by its snowy abundance. I had never seen hair so full and so pure, and I wondered if some sort of spell had turned his hair this color. My admiration for his hair was undoubtedly directly linked to my unwitting association of it with Santa Claus' plumage. Both were magical, in my opinion.

I remember vividly creating a story of origin about the color of my grandfather's hair. The story went like this: He was climbing the Rocky Mountains in the dead of winter when the wind blew off his ski cap. He saved himself by creating a makeshift hat out of the fur of a wild mountain lion he had killed just before it attacked a defenseless baby goat. Unfortunately, by the time he had sewn together the mountain lion cap, the cold had already frozen all of the color out of his hair.

Honestly, I really wish I had written it down and mailed the story to myself, because I would have serious grounds for a copyright lawsuit against Disney's *Frozen*. But that's beside the point.

The story of Umpa's magical hair just made too much sense to not be true. I believed it, in fact, until Christmas Eve, 1998, when I was simultaneously fed two bits of devastating information: Umpa's hair was not, in fact, magical but had turned white from age and Santa Claus's hair wasn't magical either because Santa Claus wasn't even real. That was not a banner day in the life of young Jedidiah Hartley.

But after I became aware that my grandfather's hair did not have magical powers, I still greatly admired it. I think that for every gray hair on a person's head, there is a good story to go along with it. And if a gray hair represents a good story, then a white hair must represent a great one. I look forward to the day when I can point to a white hair of mine and tell my great-grandchildren, "Hey, let me tell you about what gave me this one."

Admittedly, it is a bit difficult imagining my grandfather as anything different from the picture I just described to you. I was born well after his years in the military, his many odd jobs, and his many years as a principal. So when he would tell me stories of his past, regardless of his age in the story, I only envisioned an old man with white hair, a kind smile, a subtle temperament, and an incredible mind. The dozens of chess games we played are engraved inside of me, creating a perception of my grandfather as a brilliant (when he would trounce me) and a gracious (when he would let me win) man.

Pictures of my grandfather as a young man didn't help much, either. There was only about a decade where photography and his hair both possessed color. When I looked at photos of my grandfather as a young man, I still saw only Umpa.

As my grandfather aged, poor health robbed him of certain glow in his appearance. His cheery smile became rather infrequent, and his incredible mind was not nearly as sharp. "I don't want to remember him like this," I told my dad after one particular visit to the hospital. My grandfather was so disoriented and in so much pain that he could hardly speak.

"I know Jed…but you've got to understand that illness can sometimes make someone different from whom they truly are," my dad said, his voice trailing off a bit as he got lost in memories. For a few moments, he didn't say anything. But then he continued: "You know, your grandfather used to always tell me, 'don't judge a book by its cover.' I say, don't judge a book until you've read every chapter." Dad smiled. "We think we know who people are because we have read a few sentences of their life. There are many chapters to someone's story. Don't be the one who sets down the book just before it gets good."

For a second, Dad paused, pondering the wisdom of his father.

"He always taught me to believe in people, and to never let the beginning of someone's book keep you from reading on. You know, I think the same principle applies for endings. As confusing, difficult, or painful an ending might be, you should never forget the beauty of the story that unfolded on the pages before it." Dad seemed to be speaking these words of encouragement to himself, as well as to me.

— - - —

John Hartley had a knack for taking a bad situation and making something good out of it. Often during his many years as principal of Bancroft School, issues arose that would have overwhelmed most people, but John possessed a calm and fatherly disposition that gave him the ability to approach tough situations with grace. And thanks to the rambunctious individuals he had under his own roof, he was no stranger to challenges.

One of the most daunting challenges John ever faced was a student named Latisha. Fourteen-year-old Latisha transferred to Bancroft after being expelled from her previous school. She was tough and angry with a history of beating up kids, young and old alike. She struggled academically but never asked for help because she didn't want to show weakness. She had a spotty attendance record, to say the least, and most of her teachers were relieved when she didn't show up for the day. Despite John's creative ability to dream up solutions to any problem, he was finding it difficult to think of a way to help Latisha. She was bad news and there was no way around it.

The school finally reached its limit with Latisha when she got into a fight with a couple of older boys. Latisha had given both of them black eyes and was beating them handily when the fight was stopped by a faculty member, to the boys' relief.

The school board decided that if they could not figure out some way to keep her in line, she would have to be expelled. Many were ready to expel her right then and there, but John persuaded them to give her one more chance. He wondered how much of Latisha's violence was rooted in her own fear and insecurity from never feeling as if someone else believed in her. He thought that things might change if someone took the time to notice and value her.

He approached Latisha after school one day and asked her to join him in his office. She grumbled and reluctantly followed, assuming that she was in trouble for something. But as she got to his office, she was met by the warm smiles of John and several other faculty members. John handed her a golden badge and said, "Latisha, we are giving you a promotion!"

John had arranged for Latisha to be assigned as a student teacher for three first-graders.

"These students need you," he said, "and they are now your responsibility. I know you are going to do a great job." He had such excitement and certainty, Latisha couldn't help but believe him. Not quite knowing what to say, she took the badge and smiled.

"I'll give it my best, Mr. Hartley," she said.

Many of the other teachers only saw trouble arising from giving a girl like Latisha responsibility, and not just any responsibility, but the charge of young and impressionable children! But John had a dangerous sense of hope, and he saw something inside of Latisha that many others didn't see.

Latisha quickly bonded with the first graders and, when she found out a few of her kids were getting bullied by a second grader, she decided to teach this bully a lesson. John nearly had to take back the badge when he found the young boy tied to the flag pole.

"You can't do things like that!" John admonished.

"It's alright, Mr. Hartley. I wasn't going to leave him there. He just needed a time-out," Latisha said dismissively.

John sighed. It wasn't a great start but at least she was trying to do something right.

The more Latisha bonded with her students, the more she began to open up. Many of her children would come to her for help with their homework, but Latisha hardly knew how to read and write herself, so she had to humble herself and go to her teachers for help. It wasn't instantaneous, but slowly and surely, Latisha began to change.

At the end of the year, Latisha came to John with tears in her eyes. Her family was moving, and she was going to have to enroll in a different school. John told her how sad he was to see her go but assured her that she had an incredible future. She did not say much but handed him a cake that she had baked.

When he got home, John found a note beneath the cake, thanking him for believing in her and giving her an opportunity to change. John took the note and showed it to his family. With a sparkle in his eye, he said, "Look, none of the words are misspelled."

6

FIXING THE SEAWALL

John Hartley was a man of simple tastes and minimal possessions. Being the provider for a family of five on a paltry principal's salary, frugality was a necessity. However, even if he had brought home a six-figure income and was living on his own, it would not have changed much—he would have still counted his change and simplified his expenses.

He was not cheap. He merely had an intrinsic sense of value and knew better than to be wasteful. He taught at a school where many of the families rarely had enough money to put bread on the table, and he saw firsthand how a couple of dollars could change someone's life.

One day, while walking into school, John saw one of his students, Xavier, sitting on the back stoop of the school, crying. John had to do a double take to confirm that it was, in fact, Xavier. Xavier was a tough young man who rarely showed weakness, much less tearing up in public. John approached the young man and, with a fatherly comfort, asked him what was wrong.

A bit embarrassed, Xavier stiffened and cleared his voice before responding.

"Well, Mr. Hartley, it's just that…well, it's my sister's day to wear the shoes."

John had not noticed before, but he looked down to see that Xavier was not wearing shoes. The boy explained that his family could not afford shoes, so his father had provided one pair of hand-me-down shoes for Xavier and his sister to share.

"And see, they won't let me in school if I ain't got shoes," Xavier explained.

John reached into his coat pocket without hesitation and pulled out a couple of dollar bills and some change and handed it to Xavier.

"I want you to go down to the thrift store and buy yourself some shoes."

Concerned that the boy wouldn't be able to get anything with the small amount of money he had given him, John checked his pockets for any more money but came up empty. A couple dollars and change would have to do.

"I'll call the thrift store and let them know you're coming," John said, as Xavier took the money and bounded off.

A couple hours later, with no sign of Xavier, he began to worry if he had decided to take off with the money. It wouldn't have been that far-fetched of a notion; most of John's students grew up having to steal to survive, so handing out money to any of them was a high-risk investment.

John hopped on the phone and called the thrift store clerk.

"I called earlier about Xavier, who was looking to buy some shoes. Has he come by yet?"

"He just left, actually," the clerk responded.

"Didn't he arrive over an hour ago? What was he doing there so long?"

The clerk chuckled. "Well, the kid was so excited that he had to try on all the shoes we had so he knew he was buying the perfect pair."

As the clerk was finishing his sentence, John looked out the window to see Xavier returning, a smile on his face, a pair of blue Nike shoes on his feet, and a smaller pink pair strung up over his shoulder. John cracked a grin as he thanked the clerk and hung up the phone. As Xavier walked into the school, John met him in the hallway. Xavier lifted up the pink shoes and held them proudly.

"Well, Xavier, that's great, but I'm not sure how much good they will do you; they look a little small," John joked.

Xavier kicked up his feet showing off his new blue Nikes.

"Nah, Mr. Hartley, these are mine. They gave me a buy one/get one free deal. The pink ones are for my sister," Xavier said with a contagious smile.

"Well, they look good, Xavier. Now you better go catch the last bit of class."

He handed Xavier a note explaining his absence and sent him down the hall. But, as Xavier got halfway down the hall, he stopped and turned back.

"Oh, Mr. Hartley," Xavier said, as he ran back down the hallway. "Here's your change." Xavier pulled out a dollar and twenty-five cents from his pocket and handed it to John.

"Like I said, they gave me a good deal."

From that day forward, John always collected change, because he knew that a couple of extra dollars could make all the difference to someone in need.

So when John did make a purchase outside of the basic necessities, it was quite a big deal. The biggest purchase he ever made was a small summer lake house on Lake Lotawana. He had received money from the government as compensation for contracting polio while serving in the military. John wasn't much for handouts, so he took only a small portion to pay for his medical bills. With the little extra he had left over, he bought the Lotawana lake house.

The house was a small and humble, barely big enough to hold the seven-member Hartley family. But it had a big back yard with a little dock out on the lake and, for John, it was a place of freedom, a breath of fresh air, and a break from the worries and challenges of everyday life. Every summer as Bobby was growing up, John would rally the family and take them to the lake house for a couple of weeks at a time.

When they first bought the house, John's wife, Ann, immediately decided that it needed freshening up. She bought several cans of turquoise paint, her favorite color, and proceeded to paint the house. She might have gotten a bit carried away, because she ended up covering every inch of that house with turquoise—the inside walls, the exterior walls, the celling, the deck, even the toilet seats. Unfortunately for Bobby, he found out about the freshly painted toilet seats the hard way.

Bobby was always a bit disappointed when it was time to head to the lake. He had to leave all of his friends at home in order to cram into a small lake house with his brothers and sisters. On top of everything, Bobby hated turquoise. After a few days of playing out on the lake, however, Bobby always warmed up to it.

One day, when Bobby was out swimming with his brothers, a man by the name of Lenny O'Neal drove up in a brand new pontoon boat and tied it to the Hartley's dock. Lenny, a young lawyer, had been good friends with Bobby's dad for quite some time, so it was not uncommon for him to drop by. Lenny, however, didn't live on the lake or own a boat, so Bobby was a bit perplexed as Lenny pulled up.

"Hey, Bobby, come help me tie this thing up, will you?" Lenny asked, as he began fastening a rope to the end of the boat.

Bobby pulled himself out of the water and trotted over to help.

"Tie this to that hook on the seawall," Lenny said, as he tossed Bobby the other end of the rope.

"Whose boat is this?" Bobby asked, tugging hard on the rope and making the knot as secure as possible.

"It's your dad's!" Lenny exclaimed with a cheery smile. "He just doesn't know it yet."

Bobby dropped his jaw in shock. Bobby knew his dad had wanted a pontoon boat for quite some time, but he just never had the money for it.

"You bought my dad a boat?" Bobby nearly shouted with excitement.

"Sure did!" Lenny said, matching Bobby's tone.

Bobby and his brothers gawked at the new boat. They had never had anything so nice and so new.

"What are you guys waiting for?" Lenny asked. "Let's go get your dad."

Without a moment's hesitation, the three boys raced toward the house, knocking each other over as they tumbled through the back door. John, who was sitting in the house reading, leapt up, startled. Bobby grabbed his dad and began to drag him outside.

"Dad, come outside! We have to show you something!"

John followed Bobby warily. The boy's excitement was suspicious, and John figured they had hatched some elaborate plot to prank him as soon as he stepped outside. He moved slowly and cautiously.

"Hurry up, Dad!" Bobby yelled in near hysteria.

John stepped out the doorway and met eyes with Lenny, who was beaming with a smile that reached ear to ear.

"Mr. O'Neal bought you a boat!" Bobby blurted out.

John's eyes shot toward the dock, and he nearly fell over when he saw the new pontoon boat sitting there.

"That dock just looked too lonely sitting there without a boat," Lenny said, as he slapped John on the back. Still trying to comprehend what had been given to him, John stood speechless.

"Well," Lenny said, "you should probably take her for a spin."

Within seconds, John traversed the distance to the boat and was turning the keys in the ignition. By this time, Bobby's mother and sisters had come out to see what all the commotion was about. Bobby explained to them what had happened, and his mother immediately burst into tears. She hugged Lenny as tightly as she could and thanked him profusely. But the Hartley's' celebration came to an abrupt halt when they heard a large crack.

John had been so excited to drive off in his new pontoon that he had forgotten to untie it from the seawall. Bobby looked over just in time to see the boat lurch forward, breaking the seawall and sending it tumbling into the lake. Bobby and Lenny rushed down to the lake and assessed the damage. The seawall had been totally destroyed, and the boat had even broken part of the dock. Bobby looked up at his dad who had quickly killed the motor. Immediately aware of what he had just done, John dropped his head in defeat.

For a few moments no one said anything. Bobby had never seen his father so dejected. John was normally strong-spirited and held himself with such a confident stature that you would never see him succumb to a hopeless moment. But this failure weighed heavily on John's spirit, his demeanor betraying the disappointment and shame that had welled up inside of his chest. He got off the boat and without a word, headed up the path toward the house.

Lenny and the rest of the family slowly dispersed, leaving Bobby alone on the dock. Normally, Bobby was too consumed with his own troubles and mischief for him to feel the weight of another's burden. But Bobby had always loved and looked up to his father, and it troubled him to see his dad so dejected. Bobby looked toward the new pontoon boat floating next to the broken seawall and wished mightily that he had warned his dad or done something to prevent the accident.

Bobby stood over the crumbled seawall. Most of it had fallen into the lake, and the part of the wall that still stood had cracks running across its entire foundation. Bobby jumped into the lake, swam down to the bottom, and was surprised to find that the lake was only about eight feet deep along the wall. Realizing that he could easily reach the broken pieces on the lake bottom, Bobby decided to retrieve as many as he could and put the seawall back together.

For the next few hours, Bobby dove to the bottom of the lake, picked up slabs of broken concrete, and then placed them in empty cavities in the wall. But the more he tried, the more it became apparent that this was a hopeless cause. As soon as a slab bore the weight of another slab, they both would tumble back down to the bottom of the lake. Often, he dropped a piece before he was able to place it and had to surface for air. Many of the slabs were much too big for him to pick up, and even if he were able to lift them, the wall wouldn't have any more structural integrity than a pile of gravel. But the picture of his father hanging his head in disappointment stuck in Bobby's mind, fueling him to keep trying. He spent every bit of effort he could muster trying to reassemble the seawall and, at the end of the day, it was no better off than when Bobby began.

As it started getting dark, Bobby finally gave up and crawled onto the deck to catch his breath. As he glanced up toward his house, he was surprised to see his dad standing about a hundred feet up the trail. He stood there with hands in his pockets and a profound smile on his face. He had come out to assess how much it would cost to fix the wall and had stopped when he saw Bobby trying put the wall back together. Watching his son work caused him to forget about the trouble. He no longer cared about the broken wall; he didn't care about the money it would take to fix it; he didn't care that Bobby wasn't actually making any progress. All he cared about in that moment was Bobby, and how his son was trying so hard to care for his heart.

7

"FOR THE TEAM!"

It has been more than thirty years since my dad last wrestled competitively, and yet the sport is still as much a part of him now as it was back then. The only difference is that when he was in high school, wrestling took place on a mat with other wrestlers; now, it can take place anywhere and with absolutely anyone. Dad has developed a tendency to suddenly, and without warning, snap into attack mode; it doesn't matter if you are sprightly young man or an eighty-five-year-old senior, you may soon find yourself on the floor with burly arms twisting your limbs in ways you weren't ever aware they could twist.

Wrestling is, and has always been, a foundational part of his identity. As the saying goes, you can take the lion out of the jungle but you can't take the jungle out of the lion. I used to wonder why he was still so competitive, but as I now look back on my Dad's upbringing it begins to make more sense.

When Bobby started wrestling in his early teens he was going through some foundational shifts in his life. His early appetite for adventure was quickly turning into teenage restlessness. He struggled with the line between ambition and aggression and rarely knew what do with himself. To make it worse, his family changed neighborhoods. Drug and gang influences had begun to creep into St. Catherine's Gardens, and the once kid-heaven was now teeming with negative influences. Bobby was pulled out of the Catholic school he had grown up in and enrolled in a public high school—a jarring transition, to say the least. He went from a strict, nun-ruled school to the chaos and disarray of the public school system.

On Bobby's first day of school he saw a group of "greasers" flip a parked Volkswagen onto its side. He figured they must have really hated the owner. Later he realized they didn't have a clue who owned it, they just enjoyed breaking stuff. It took several months for Bobby to grow accustomed to his new surroundings, and just as he was beginning to find a place within the school, a group of kids stole some expensive glass beakers from the science lab. When questioned, they blamed Bobby—the new kid and an easy target. Bobby, impetuous as always and upset about the accusations, jumped on one of the kids in the middle of class, wrestling him down and twisting his arm in an attempt to provoke a confession. The school principal was less than pleased with Bobby's antics and promptly expelled him, forcing Bobby to join yet another school, Hickman Mills.

So when Bobby began wrestling it quickly became more than just a sport for him; it became a way of handling life. Each time he would step onto the mat, he would look at his opponent and see the embodiment of all the challenges life had begun to throw his way. Every issue he could not handle, every problem he could not solve, stood before him. When the bell rang to start the round, he would wage war against all of them. Despite the blood and bruises, the intense and even masochistic training, it was exhilarating for Bobby. In a world full of things beyond his grasp and comprehension, he had discovered something he could control.

A wrestler only competes with opponents within his own weight class, so a wrestler's goal is to be as strong and tough as possible while also weighing as little as possible. When Bobby joined the wrestling team, he changed the way he ate, the way he worked out, and even the way he slept, all in an attempt to gain muscle mass while also losing weight. He developed a habit of wearing thick sweatpants and sweatshirts covered by a plastic track suit so that, whenever he would do any sort of physical exercise, he would "sweat out" as much water weight as possible. Before tournament weigh-ins, Bobby would even sleep in his many-layered sweats in an attempt to "make weight" the next morning.

Due to his tenacity, Bobby became a rather dominant wrestler. However, the rest of his team at Hickman Mills was hardly as emphatic about the sport. The wrestling program was small, and the coach was in his first year and hardly knew a thing about wrestling. Most of Bobby's teammates were poorly trained and fairly un-athletic. The least athletic of the team was a young boy from India named Amit.

Bobby never could figure out why Amit had joined the wrestling team. He was neither physically gifted nor aggressive. In fact, he was just about the least competitive individual Bobby had ever met. When practicing, Amit would practically pin himself. His opponent only needed to act like he was going to dominate, and Amit would immediately wilt. During tournaments, Bobby and some of the other boys would bet on how long it would take Amit to get pinned. There was never a doubt in their minds that he was going to get pinned—the only question was how long it would take.

Amit's family had moved to the United States from New Delhi, India. Amit's English was rough, which, along with his lack of athletic prowess, made him a prime target for jokes and mockery. But Amit didn't take the jeering to heart and, due to his blissful and cordial spirit, had soon made friends with most of the wrestling team. Bobby wondered if the whole reason Amit had joined the wrestling team was an odd attempt at making new friends. All Bobby really knew was that Amit certainly did not join the team with the intention of winning matches.

As the year wore on Amit eventually became a beloved part of the wrestling team and everyone would gather around to cheer him on during his matches. Everyone, that is, except for Bobby. Despite how likeable Amit was, Bobby had a hard time connecting with him. Wrestling was a big deal to Bobby and Amit treated it like a joke. A few times Bobby even tried to teach Amit better form, but it was useless. Amit just didn't have any fight in him. And that was something Bobby had a hard time looking past. But another thing that rubbed Bobby the wrong way was how Amit's father attended every one of the team's tournaments. *Why does he always come?* Bobby wondered as he watched Amit's father come down from the stands and congratulate his son after a match. The congratulations didn't make sense: Amit was a horrible wrestler!

Bobby's own father hardly ever came to watch the tournaments; wrestling was too violent for John Hartley. His gentle spirit had a hard time condoning its fierce nature. Even if he did come, he wouldn't say much after the match. Bobby was frustrated to see Amit receive more praise for failing than Bobby ever seemed to receive for succeeding.

During the last tournament of the year, Hickman Mills had actually accumulated enough points to contend for seventh place.

With only eight teams competing in the tournament, seventh place was nothing to brag about, but they had placed dead last in every tournament leading up to this one, and they all desperately wanted to finish, just once, above last.

Doing some quick math, Bobby realized they were still two points away from seventh place, with only one match remaining. Two points were fairly easy to get in a match; all a wrestler had to do was avoid getting pinned, and he would be awarded at least a few points. The only problem was that the last match left was Amit's.

When Bobby realized this, he shook his head and headed straight for the locker room. He couldn't watch; he already knew the outcome. Amit had wrestled in thirteen previous matches that year and not once had he made it past the first round. But before Bobby even got to the locker room, one of his teammates grabbed him.

"Hartley, you've got to see this!" he said.

Bobby could hear the crowd cheering. It was only a minute into the first round and Amit's opponent already had him on his back. Amit fought hard, doing absolutely everything in his power to keep from getting pinned. His opponent, an experienced wrestler, was pressuring Amit with excellent technique and, several times, nearly had him pinned, but Amit would turn and contort his body, enduring an incredible amount of pain, all in a desperate effort to keep the match going.

Bobby had never seen Amit try so hard. In fact, Bobby had never really seen Amit try at all. Amit had been told that Hickman Mills would place seventh as long as he lasted all three rounds without getting pinned. Before stepping onto the mat, Amit had looked at his coach and in his thick Indian accent said, "For the team!"

The crowd went crazy as the buzzer sounded the end of the first round, but everyone quickly hushed as they watched Amit struggle to stand up and get off the mat. He was in such excruciating pain that a couple of his teammates had to help him off. On the opposite end of the mat, the coach of Amit's opponent chastised his wrestler for letting the match go to a second round. With two full rounds remaining, Bobby half-expected Amit to throw in the towel. He had already exceeded every expectation; there was no need to go back out there for only seventh place. But Amit's eyes lifted to the crowd, and Bobby followed his gaze to see Amit's father beaming with an ear-to-ear smile. Amit collected himself and mustered the courage and strength to return to the mat for the second round. Just before he went out, Amit looked at his coach and then to Bobby, and repeated, "For the team!"

As the second round started, Amit's opponent almost immediately had him in a position worse than any he had endured through the first round. His arms were locked and his opponent was attempting to roll him forward onto his back. Without the use of his arms, all Amit could do to keep from flipping was dig his face into the mat. If he ducked his head under, his opponent could easily roll Amit onto his back for an instant pin. So Amit kept his head planted on the mat and endured the strain on his neck and the pain from the friction between his face and the mat.

Determined to flip him, Amit's opponent began to twist on his arm, putting more and more pressure on it. Just before the end of the second round, Bobby heard a loud *pop*. The opponent loosened his grip as Amit screamed in pain. Amit had dislocated his shoulder. The buzzer sounded the end of the second round and Amit was helped off the mat once again.

By this time, the crowd had stopped watching the other matches and had all moved over to watch this little Indian boy fight for seventh place. They even paused the first-place match so that everyone could watch. Bobby looked up towards Amit's father in the crowded stands, who sat with his head hanging low and his eyes towards the floor. He could not bear to watch his son endure so much pain. But as Amit limped back onto the mat, his father slowly lifted his head and made eye contact with Amit. Through tears, Amit smiled and stood up for the final round.

Bobby, along with many others on the team, told their coach to stop the match, but Amit refused. "One more round," he said, "for the team."

The last round seemed to crawl by as the entire building watched in near silence as Amit, with a dislocated shoulder, tried desperately to stay off his back. Once again, Amit's opponent had him nearly pinned through the entire round. Bobby even thought that Amit was legally pinned a couple times during the match and wondered if perhaps the referee didn't have the heart to slap the mat. Still, Amit continued to twist and fight with more strength than he ever knew he had, and, for the third and final time, the buzzer sounded and the match was over at last. Amit had avoided the pin, giving his team barely enough points to place second-to-last in a small high school tournament. Yet, by the way the crowd reacted, you would've thought Amit had just won a gold medal at the Olympics.

If you were to look at Amit's record on paper, you would see a 0–14 record, thirteen losses by pins and one loss by major decision. That's not very impressive. But, to Amit, to Amit's father, to the entire Hickman Mills wrestling team, and to Bobby Hartley, it was much, much more.

When the season ended, the entire team, including Bobby, voted Amit the Wrestler of the Year. He may not have had a notch in the win column, but he had won the respect of this teammates and had fought harder than anyone Bobby had ever seen before.

8

FAMILY TOASTS

Bobby's competitive drive and ability to wrestle through life wasn't enough, however, to cope with the subtler challenges happening inside his family as he hit high school. I'm not sure what constitutes as a "functional" family, but to say Bobby grew up in one would be a far stretch of the imagination. However, what good does "functional" serve if you have no love for one another? Disorder and chaos ran free amid the Hartley family. But in the constant maelstrom of disorder, there were always rays of love that split through.

In Bobby's late teenage years, however, his family took an unexpected blow when his mother, Ann, was involved in a terrible accident that left her bedridden.

Ann had thrown out her back trying to restrain their family dog, a rambunctious hundred-pound mutt named Dolly, from attacking the mailman. Ann had grabbed Dolly's chain and pulled it taut with such force, it caused Dolly to flip backwards.

Bobby, sitting on the deck, watched it unfold. He was amazed by his mother's strength; she was a fairly small woman, but by the way Dolly had snapped back you would have thought the dog had been chained to a brick wall. Bobby was about to remark on his mother's outstanding power when he saw her double over in pain. The force had ruptured a disc in her back.

That week, Ann was in so much agonizing discomfort, Bobby's father took her to the hospital to get emergency reconstructive back surgery. While operating on what should have been an uncomplicated procedure, the doctor accidentally nicked Ann's sciatic nerve with his scalpel. When she got out of surgery, the pain was excruciating—far worse than what she had felt before, and this time nothing could be done.

The cut on her nerve became a source of constant suffering for Ann. Anytime she stood up or was at all mobile, the pain would flare up to unbearable levels. She was forced to spend most of her days confined to her bed. The physical anguish began to change Ann; her personality and disposition took a turn for the worse. Her medications made her moods unpredictable. The constant discomfort set her on edge, making it easy for her to lose her temper. And the general restlessness and loneliness of remaining in bed almost every day nearly drove her crazy.

For Bobby, who didn't understand the pain his mother was going through, it was all very confusing and frustrating. His mother had always been a source of joy and life, but she was now distant and angry. She often lashed out at her own family, and it seemed as if that anger had seeped into the family's core. His home had been chaotic before, but it always full of life, joy, and warmth as well. Now it had grown cold, and the love replaced with pain.

On Christmas morning of Bobby's senior year in high school, all Bobby could think about was how long it would be before he could ditch his family's celebration to be with his friends.

Bobby had started working for a roofing company run by a man named Lenny Schmidt. Lenny had a son named Jim, who was just a few years older than Bobby, and whenever Bobby was not at school or at work, he was with Jim. They would sneak into bars looking for either a fight or a drink—and often finding both. Only seventeen years old at the time, Bobby wasn't old enough to drink, but he found that if he walked in with the rest of the roofing crew, no one ever gave him any trouble.

Bobby was planning on joining the guys to get a drink later that Christmas Day, but for now he was stuck with his family.

They had just finished eating a rather meager Christmas lunch and were now headed to the living room to unwrap the gag gifts they always got one another. Ann had left the family in a fit of anger and locked herself in her bedroom. She rarely felt well enough to leave her bedroom in the first place, so Bobby had been surprised just to see her for breakfast. What she was angry about he could only guess. It seemed as if anything could set her off those days.

"A toast to Dad!" Kathy said as she grabbed her glass and raised it high.

It had become a tradition for the kids to toast their father on Christmas morning. However the toasts were more in jest than in respect. "Here's to the fact he only lost six sets of keys this year!" one would say. "Hear, hear!" the rest would respond and clink their glasses. Each year it got more and more elaborate as they found bigger and better jokes. Sometimes they would tell a story, other times they would write a poem, but it always was a tribute to something foolish or clumsy their father had done that year.

John Hartley was a brilliant man, but he had a way of occasionally overlooking general principles of common sense. Contrasted with the wise demeanor he regularly held, these momentary slip-ups and oversights made him a target for jest. But far from being offended by the jokes, he was often amused by his own absent-minded mistakes.

Kathy was the oldest of the family. As a quick-witted and articulate communicator, she always spearheaded the toasting tradition and prepared the most eloquent "toasts." She pulled out a piece of paper and began to read a speech she had prepared.

"A toast to the man who almost drowned himself," she pronounced as she shook her head:

> John Hartley, John Hartley. When he found out drinking water was good for you,
>
> He went to the store and bought a gallon jug of water, then he went back and bought two.
>
> John Hartley, John Hartley. He drank and he drank that water all day,
>
> "You can never get too much of a good thing," he would say.
>
> Well, John Hartley, John Hartley, I'm afraid you were wrong.
>
> Apparently you can drown yourself if you drink gallons all day long!

True to the poem, John had nearly drowned himself that year by drinking too much water—a silly mistake that almost cost him dearly. He had passed out while at work and was taken to the hospital to be treated for "water intoxication."

Kathy cleared her throat and continued:

John Hartley, John Hartley. Only a man like our dad,

Could ever almost kill himself from something so sad.

John Hartley, John Hartley....

Kathy stopped mid-sentence. She began to get choked up. She crumpled up her paper and let it drop to the ground as a tear escaped from her eye.

"I'm sorry," Kathy said, trying hard to keep her composure. "I don't want to make fun."

Looking straight at her dad she shook her head.

"I was scared when you had to go to the hospital...I...well, I just can't imagine life without you. You are an amazing man and I've learned so much from you." Her words were uncharacteristically wholehearted. It just wasn't like Kathy, or any of the Hartleys, to speak so vulnerably. They were a family that loved each other deeply but rarely communicated it very clearly.

"One day, I hope I can grow up to marry a man just like you."

Kathy walked over and gave her father a hug and then stepped back and wiped her tears.

Billy, the second oldest in the family, who always followed his sister with his own toast, was now looking down at his notepaper uncomfortably. He too crumpled the paper and looked straight into John's eyes.

"Dad, she's right. You are a good man, and a good father."

Bobby felt tears welling up in his own eyes. The words seemed so sincere, and Bobby didn't quite know how to handle such sincerity. He shifted in his seat, uncomfortably trying his best not to cry in front of his family.

"I'm not going to joke either, because the truth is…I couldn't have asked for a better father," Billy continued as he began to choke up. "When I grow up I want to be a man just like you."

And at those words Bobby got up and walked out of the house. It was far too emotional of a moment for him to stand. Besides, his toast was next, and these were acts he knew he could not follow.

9

LEAVING HOME

John always insisted that the family come together as often as possible for dinner, and every so often things would seem to calm down enough that the home would once again feel like a place of safety and joy.

During one such night, the whole family sat in the living room after dinner to watch the latest Perry Mason episode, a collective favorite. It was refreshing for Bobby to feel comfortable inside of his home, and for a moment he relaxed. Then Ann bent down to pick up a few books left out on the floor, causing her back pain to flare up, and she began to yell angrily at her children.

Bobby, infuriated at his mother's unreasonable anger, began to argue with her. Ann went back to her room and slammed the door in Bobby's face. He was so upset he struck the door with his fist. It broke open and swung hard into his mother, knocking her to the ground.

The rest of the family had moved into the kitchen and stood quietly, pained by the altercation. Bobby knew he had gone too far and could no longer control himself. He walked into the kitchen to see his father standing silently by the stove.

"I know I need to leave," Bobby said with a tremor in his voice.

John didn't say anything, but just stood above the gas stove, clicking it on and off, watching the flame dance up and then die down.

"Can you just tell me…why does she have to be like this?" Bobby asked, trying desperately to make sense of his mother's anger.

At first John didn't respond and just continued to click the stove on and off.

"Bobby, come here." John eventually replied with a calm voice. "Put your hand above the stove."

Bobby walked over and placed his hand above the open flame.

"What do you feel?" John asked.

"I feel pain," Bobby responded.

"Don't take it away just yet." John said. And then after a brief moment he asked again, "Bobby, what do you feel?"

"More pain!" Bobby said with just a twinge of anger in his voice. John clicked off the burner.

"Bobby, your mother is in pain, and she can't take her hand away," John said as he placed a reassuring hand on his son and looked him directly in the eyes. "I know your mother, and I know this pain is making her someone she is not. But I promised to love her all of her life when I married her, and I plan on keeping that promise. Whether she ever gets better or not, I will never stop loving her."

Bobby took his dad's hand off his shoulder and began to walk away.

"Dad," he said, "I just don't have that kind of love."

As Bobby walked out of the front door of his house, he had nothing but the clothes on his back. He had no idea where he was going to stay or even how he was going to get there—he just knew he had to go. Billy, Bobby's older brother, had watched the entire event unfold and followed Bobby outside. Without saying a word, Billy handed Bobby the keys to his car. Billy was a young man of outstanding generosity, and seeing his little brother's need, he didn't even think twice before giving Bobby his car.

After driving around for a bit, Bobby realized that he had no place to go. So he parked the car in the middle of an empty parking lot and did his best to get some sleep. The next day was the hardest of his life. He went to school and acted as if everything was completely normal. He didn't want to seem weak, and any intense emotion besides anger made him far too vulnerable. He had always carried himself with a bit of a chip on his shoulder so it was not hard for him to hide behind his anger. For the next few weeks, Bobby continued to live out of his car, and he would have continued indefinitely if it were not for Aunt May.

Bobby's well-beloved Aunt May was actually a great-aunt, in her late seventies, who lived in a nice little house in the southern Kansas City suburbs. She had never married; in fact, the closest she had ever gotten to marriage was a long time ago with a fine young man by the name of Walt Disney. Aunt May never married Walt because her father would not consent to the relationship.

"Stay away from him, May, the guy listens to a talking mouse," her father warned, and Aunt May obeyed.

A devout Catholic, she spent more time on her knees than on her feet. For the life of him, Bobby could never figure out how she had so much to pray about. She had a gentle and welcoming temperament, and a kitchen that was as inviting as her smile. She worked at Russell Stover Chocolates and would often find a way to bring some of the goods home with her. Her always comfortable home smelled perpetually of rich, delicious chocolate and Sanka instant coffee, her morning vice.

One afternoon, shortly after he had left his home, Bobby walked out of school to see Aunt May sitting in the parking lot. After exchanging brief hellos, Aunt May cut to the chase.

"Bobby, I'm sorry you had to leave your home. Would you please come and stay with me?"

Bobby was touched.

"Thank you, Aunt May. But trust me, you don't want a guy like me in your house."

"Oh stop it. Don't think I don't know what I am getting myself into," she said. "Besides, I could use some excitement. The house has been a bit boring as of late."

The thought of living in such a peaceful place put a smile on Bobby's face. He nodded. "Thank you. And I promise I won't be there for long. I'll leave as soon as I find another place."

"You can stay as long as you want," she confidently replied.

During his stay with Aunt May, Bobby would spend most of the day either at school or at work and then would party with Jim and his other coworkers. The roofing guys were rough, many of them members of biker gangs and almost all of them addicted to drugs or alcohol. Despite being some of the meanest, toughest guys Bobby had ever been around, they treated him like family and didn't care how screwed up he was. So Bobby spent almost every night with them, not returning until early hours in the morning.

Bobby, always adventurous, was now stretching beyond just thrill-seeking into near-suicidal. In South Kansas City there was a bridge being constructed that ran several hundred feet above a large rock quarry. Often Bobby and Jim would see who could walk farther on top of the railing that ran alongside of the road. The railing was a round bar with a diameter no thicker than seven or eight inches. Bobby and Jim would walk as far as a hundred feet across the rail, sometimes drunk. If they slipped too far to the right, they would have fallen to their death. Many times they came close, but they couldn't care less.

Each night Bobby left to go partying, Aunt May would sit on her porch swing and wait there, praying, until Bobby returned. She did this not to reprimand him, or even make him feel guilty, but because she cared deeply and was worried that he would not return.

One night, when Bobby was returning after a full night of drinking and partying, he could hear Aunt May praying while she sat on her porch. He felt so ashamed of how he kept going out, knowing fully how much it worried her. So in the interest of evading her, he hid underneath the bushes outside of her house, hoping she would get tired and go inside. But Aunt May continued to pray with a seemingly tireless conviction.

"Heavenly Father, thank you for Bobby. Thank you for who he is going to become. Thank you for the things he is going to do," Aunt May prayed as she rocked back and forth on her porch swing.

Bobby listened to Aunt May speak of his destiny, his future, and his worth. He turned and buried his face into the ground so she wouldn't hear him cry. He waited and waited for her to give up and go in to bed, but she never did. She continued to rock with a steady pace back and forth on the old porch swing, never ceasing her prayer while Bobby cried himself to sleep, face down in the dirt beneath the bushes.

When the sun eventually began to rise and light spilled across the lawn revealing Bobby under the bushes, Aunt May stood up from her swing, woke him, and took him inside. The two had an early morning breakfast without once mentioning the previous night. After breakfast, Aunt May decided to get some sleep and as she slept, Bobby packed up what little he had and moved out. He could not bear to burden her any longer.

10

THE INNER-CITY POOL

Over the next few months Bobby bounced around to a few different homes, staying with whomever was willing to take him in. He always left just before he was kicked out. Now graduated and working several different jobs, he figured it wouldn't be long until he could afford his own place.

Most of Bobby's workdays were spent with Lenny Schmidt's roofing company. Bobby's job was demolition, and he was good at it. The tenacity he had found as a wrestler seeped into the rest of his life, and he quickly became one of the hardest workers on the crew.

"It's Bulldog Bob time," Lenny would say as he handed Bobby the crowbar. And like the Tasmanian devil, Bobby would attack the roof in a storm and rip off as many shingles as he could until it was quitting time. The work was hard and as summer came, the sun got hotter and the days longer. Bobby wasn't getting paid much, and he knew he was worth more. He asked Lenny for a raise but Lenny just laughed and dismissed Bobby's request.

Not long after, Bobby was swimming at his own local pool with some of his buddies when a man who noticed his skill approached him and offered him a job as a lifeguard at an inner-city pool downtown. He agreed without hesitation and within a week he began working as lifeguard.

The pool was in the middle of a predominantly African-American community and when Bobby started working, he was the only Caucasian on the staff. In fact, he was really the only white person who ever went to the pool. It was the late 1960s and although the federal government had put an end to legalized segregation, Kansas City was still suffering from de facto segregation.

Most of the staff just avoided Bobby, but there were a few who went of their way to openly give him trouble. One in particular, another lifeguard named Yvette, had no problem letting Bobby know just how much she hated him. When Bobby first encountered Yvette he figured she was just about the biggest, meanest woman he had ever met. On a daily basis she would find some reason to berate both Bobby in particular and white men in general.

All of these individuals had been directly affected by the negative influences of racism so it was an understandable aggression, and Bobby knew he was waging an uphill battle. But it didn't bother Bobby one bit—he was used to being antagonized and saw it all as a challenge. He made it a point to befriend the whole staff, starting with Yvette.

After she would yell at him he would wait about fifteen minutes and then sneak up behind her and give her a big hug.

"I like you, Yvette," he would say with a sigh. He then would quickly let go and run off yelling, "One day you're going to like me, too! You can't stop it!"

It was an unconventional approach, and it really didn't do much but irritate her, but he stuck with it. He figured his kindness, albeit annoying kindness, would eventually wear her out and make her laugh, and she would give up hating him.

The job seemed pretty easy to Bobby. He spent most of his time just sitting on the lifeguard chair, spinning his whistle and seeing how high he could toss it. He wasn't getting paid much, but it was better money than demolition and not nearly as taxing.

His boss, a retired professional basketball player named Hughes always carried himself with a cool and mellow temperament. It did not take Bobby long to figure out that the source of his boss's mellow temperament was located in a glass bottle stashed beneath his office desk. But despite never being fully sober, Hughes was level-headed and ran the pool well despite its crowded chaos.

Located in the middle of a densely populated area, the pool would fill up every day with hundreds of people looking to escape the summer heat. Some days, local schools would bring busloads of kids over to the pool. And then on top of all of that, Missouri Western Mental Health Facility, a local mental institution, would occasionally bring over their patients for "aquatic therapy." Aquatic therapy was hardly as professional and intentional as it sounds; essentially, it just provided a way for the patients, who were suffering from a bevy of mental illnesses, to get outside and get some exercise. There was no form or control to any of it, the patients would just enjoy the pool for several hours and then be taken back to the institution.

"Looks like we've got ourselves a bowl of fruit loops!" one of the lifeguards would say as the patients splashed around the pool. But Bobby never laughed at the joke—for even with the amount of disarray they would cause, Bobby always enjoyed it when the patients showed up. Maybe it was from compassion, or maybe thanks to the stimulating, out-of-the-box conversations they provoked, or heck maybe it was just because he identified with such odd characters, but for whatever reason, he loved being around them.

However, the pool was underfunded, and the combination of a constant stream of children and large groups of mentally ill patients was a formula for disaster. The water was always cloudy from the amount of chlorine they had to pump into the pool to keep it at least somewhat hygienic. And even if the water was clear, the pool was full to capacity almost every day; so the lifeguards had to be constantly on the lookout.

Only about a week into working at the pool, Bobby watched a young boy and his father walk up underneath the tallest diving board. The father looked at his son and encouraged him to jump into the pool. The boy was hesitant but eventually worked up enough to courage to jump into the pool, and as soon as he hit the water he immediately sank to the bottom. Bobby paused for a second to see if the father would go in after the boy, but the father just stood there in shock helplessly watching his son drown.

Bobby jumped off of his stand, dived in the water, and tore towards the boy. As he swam down, he saw panic written all over the boy's face. Bobby reached out to grab him, but in desperation the boy clawed onto Bobby and begun shoving Bobby down to the bottom in an instinctive attempt to push himself toward the surface. Bobby knew how to swim but had never been trained in rescuing someone. For a few moments, Bobby thought he was going to drown with the boy, but his wrestling instincts kicked in and eventually he was able to lock the boy's arms to his side and swim them both to the surface.

"Why did you let him jump in if he couldn't swim?" Bobby asked the father as soon as they were both safely out of the pool.

"I didn't know this was the deep end!" he stuttered.

Bobby pointed up at the diving board.

"Yeah, they always put this on the shallow end!" Bobby said sarcastically, stunned by the father's ignorance.

Bobby was a daring young man who was hardly ever panicked or afraid, so the rare times he actually was rattled by fear, he found himself struggling to properly deal with the intense emotion that surfaced. Almost every time Bobby dove in to save someone from drowning, he would berate them for putting themselves in such a situation.

"If you don't know how to swim, stay out of the deep end!" Bobby would yell after he pulled them out of the water.

He was angered by his own fear and would lash out against the individuals whom he perceived were the instigators of such emotion. He could face adversity, that much was certain: he could wrestle whatever life threw his way and win. Enormous odds stacked against him never bothered him. When he first started working for the pool, he wasn't a bit afraid of not being liked by anyone. When in school, he wasn't afraid of getting into trouble, even with the dreaded Mr. Freed. His constant provocation of fights with people twice his size showed his lack of fear of physical pain. When he casually meandered across the I-71 rail with Jim Schmidt, hundreds of feet above the ground, he was proving to himself he wasn't even afraid of death. But when Bobby dove into the water, he was met with his real fear, the fear of failing someone.

Bobby had developed a tendency to isolate himself from those he loved most dearly, to avoid disappointing or hurting them. Even much of his trouble-making as a child could be traced to an evasion and lowering of expectations. But now Bobby was in a situation where people's very lives relied on him; they were his responsibility. The fear of failing any of them fueled an intense vigilance whenever he was on duty.

Many of the staff and those who frequented the pool took note of Bobby's intensity. A group of teenagers who frequented the pool saw how worked up Bobby would get every time he pulled someone out of the pool and found it quite amusing. So they then began to swim to the bottom of the pool and fake drowning while Bobby was on guard, just to watch him freak out.

Unamused by their games, he began getting more and more physical every time he would save someone he thought could be faking. Bobby would grab them by their hair and yank them out of the pool, sometimes even hitting them a couple times under the water, roughing them up as much as he could so that they would think twice before faking again.

But as much as Bobby's dedication and intensity drew him negative attention, it also impressed a few people. Many saw how hard Bobby would fight to save everyone, and it began to change their perception of him. By the end of the first few months, Bobby had already pulled sixteen people out of the pool. Many of the staff began to warm up to him—including Yvette. She saw the boys who would pick on Bobby and pretend to drown, and just as unamused as Bobby, she would chew them out.

"He's trying to save your lives, and you're treating him like that!" she would yell, sometimes slapping them upside the head to add extra emphasis.

Hughes also took notice of Bobby's dedication and decided to offer him a second job. Many kids had been breaking into the pool late at night, stealing things and trashing the property, so Hughes hired Bobby as a night security guard. He gave Bobby a metal baseball bat and told Bobby to chase off anyone who tried to hop the fence to get into the pool.

So Bobby would lay on one of the tables on the pool deck and fall asleep while clutching the baseball bat. He was a light sleeper and whenever anyone would try to climb the fence he would wake up and rush towards them like a rabid junkyard dog swinging wildly with the baseball bat. After the first few weeks, the kids stopped trying to break into the pool entirely, and Bobby was able to sleep peacefully through the night.

11

LITTLE WILLIE

Things were going well for Bobby; he was keeping busy with his several jobs and was even getting paid to sleep with a bat inside the pool. Hughes also began paying Bobby to run errands for him while Bobby was on his breaks. Or rather, to run one errand: Hughes would hand Bobby some cash, he would run across the block and buy a bottle of peppermint schnapps at the local liquor store, and then bring it back to Hughes.

One day when Bobby returned from a liquor run, he handed Hughes the bottle and the few dollars change he had extra. Hughes took a swig from the bottle and smiled, and as he always did when Bobby handed him the change he said, "Keep it!" with a nod and slapped Bobby on the back.

Bobby tucked the couple of dollars into his swim trunk pocket and walked out to the pool to start his shift. Bobby sighed as he looked and saw the Missouri Western Mental Health bus sitting in the parking lot. As much as he loved it when they came, it was still so much more chaotic when they were at the pool—and today was already a particularly crowded day.

Bobby nodded to the lifeguard on duty to indicate it was time to switch. He pulled out his whistle and began to twirl it as the other lifeguard got off the stand. Then, just moments after climbing up onto the stand before he even had a chance to sit down, a couple of the kids yelled out to Bobby:

"There is a boy lying at the bottom of the pool!"

Bobby's eyes shot towards the boys and then to where they were pointing, but the water was so murky and the pool was so crowded he couldn't see what they were talking about.

"Pick him up!" Bobby yelled back to the boys, wondering if they were perhaps just messing with him.

"You pick him up!" One of the boy's said, the tremor of fear in his voice telling Bobby that this was no joke.

Without a moment of hesitation, Bobby hit the water and within just a couple of strokes he was across the pool. At first Bobby didn't see anything, but then all of the sudden his eyes locked onto a small boy who lay motionless at the bottom of the pool. Bobby immediately recognized the boy; he was a sweet six-year-old with bright brown eyes, dark tight curls, and a brilliant smile. His name was William Jr. but everyone called him Little Willie.

With a greater sense of a fear and desperation than he had ever felt before, Bobby grabbed Willie and cradled him in his arms. As Bobby picked him up out of the water, Willie's head dropped back and his body went limp. Bobby searched the boy's face for any sign of life, but found none.

Bobby set Willie gently on the pool deck and looked up to see the entire pool had cleared and everyone stood pressed up against the fence. Bobby had not been trained in CPR so he had no idea what to do.

"Please, someone help!" Bobby screamed in desperation, but his cries went unanswered. Fear immobilized everyone. Even the kids and those from the mental health institute had immediately recognized what was going on. Bobby looked down at the hauntingly lifeless body of Little Willie.

Bobby started to give mouth-to-mouth to the boy but he had no idea how to perform the procedure properly. He knew his efforts were useless, but he kept trying. Eventually a woman came up out of the crowd who told Bobby she was a nurse, and she took over trying to resuscitate Little Willie. In reality, she was not a nurse, had just started going to nursing school, and didn't really know much more than Bobby.

Hughes had seen Bobby pull Willie out of the pool and immediately called 911. The ambulance arrived in just a matter of minutes, but for Bobby it seemed like an eternity. He was in a near hysteria when the paramedics arrived.

"Is he going to be okay?" Bobby yelled just they were putting Willie into the back of the ambulance, but none of the paramedics responded. They shut the doors to the ambulance and drove off to the hospital, sirens screaming. Bobby breathed deeply trying to maintain composure. He walked over to the fence and held onto it to keep himself from falling over.

The pool shut down and everyone left, except for the group of boys who liked to pick on Bobby by pretending to be drowning; they all stood on the outside of the fence. One of boys walked over to Bobby who was still clutching the other side of the fence trying to calm himself.

"You are kicking us out before closing time!" the boy said with a complete ignorance of the intensity of the situation. "Hey, are you listening to me?" he yelled at Bobby. "I want my money back, you—" He was about to call Bobby a name, but he didn't have time. The fence that had been separating Bobby and the boys was about seven feet tall and had barbed wire at the top, but Bobby had no trouble clearing it in a split second. He grabbed the boy and threw him to the ground while the boy's friends scattered in a panic.

"How could you?" Bobby screamed as he picked the boy up and threw him against the fence. "There is a six-year-old boy, probably dead, riding away in an ambulance and you're complaining about a refund!"

Hughes pulled Bobby off of the boy and told Bobby to follow him back to his office. Bobby collapsed in a chair in Hughes's office, completely wrecked. He had just felt the life slip out of Little Willie in his very own arms.

"He's...that boy's going to die, Hughes!"

"You don't know that," Hughes said shaking his head.

"I couldn't get there quick enough, I...I couldn't resuscitate him. I don't know how to." Bobby rambled on, verbally trying to make sense of what had just happened.

Hughes didn't know what to say or how to help Bobby, so he simply handed Bobby a bottle of peppermint schnapps.

Bobby had never had hard liquor before, despite his many nights with the Vauts. He took the bottle, stood up, and walked out of the office.

"Where are you going?" Hughes asked, concerned.

"I need to find out if he is okay," Bobby said as he set out walking to the hospital.

When he arrived at the hospital, he tossed the now-empty bottle into the front bushes before staggering his way through the hospital doors and up to the front desk.

"Is he okay?" Bobby asked with an ache in his voice and a slur in his speech. The nurse, confused and concerned by Bobby's drunken state, did not respond. "A little boy named Willie was brought in here and I need to know if he is okay!" Bobby emphasized.

Before the nurse had a chance to respond, a man who had overheard Bobby introduced himself.

"I am William Sr." The man said as he took Bobby's hand and shook it. "I am Willie's father."

"I am so sorry,"" Bobby said as he locked eyes with William. "It was all my fault. I was the lifeguard and I tried…I should have gotten there."

William was only in his late thirties, but life had already taken a hard toll on him, judging by his tired eyes and weathered face. But he smiled a comforting smile and spoke reassuringly to Bobby.

"It's not your fault, son." William said as he put a reassuring hand on Bobby's shoulder. William's words brought momentary stability to Bobby's crumbling world. "They took Willie into intensive care; we are waiting to hear from the doctor." William led Bobby back to the waiting room where the rest of Willie's family sat anxiously. "You can wait with us," William continued.

As Bobby looked around the room at the members of Willie's family, he began to break down in tears.

"I am so, so sorry," Bobby repeated. "I should have saved him."

Most of the family didn't know how to respond, nor did they have much time to. The doctor came into the waiting room and called the family back and Bobby was left alone staring hopelessly at the waiting room walls. They say white and green walls bring a calming effect. The walls didn't seem to be working for Bobby. He stood up and began to pace. The eerie silence of the nearly empty room weighed on Bobby until a soothing voice cut through the quite.

"Excuse me, young man."

Bobby turned to see a beautiful woman with long dark hair and gentle smile approach him. The woman looked as if she were in her mid-thirties, but as she got closer Bobby began to figure she was a bit older, early forties perhaps. She wore a trendy olive green skirt and a white blouse. Something about her presence caused Bobby to relax a bit.

"I heard you speak with that man," she said with a look of concern and keen interest. "You said it was your fault; would you mind telling me what happened?"

Bobby tried to fight back tears. He really didn't want to talk about it, but then again perhaps he did need to process it, and this woman seemed as if she truly cared. She had a sweet and understanding temperament, and at the moment Bobby desperately needed a friend. The two went outside, and Bobby wept as he told the woman everything. How he didn't know how to do CPR, how he had hesitated before jumping into the pool, and how now Little Willie might die because of him.

The woman in the olive skirt listened to Bobby intently, only interrupting every once in a while to ask the occasional question or to have Bobby expound on a certain detail. She never stopped him to say that it wasn't his fault, that he tried as hard as he could, or even that things were going to be okay. She just listened.

When Bobby had finished his story, she nodded and smiled.

"I wish you the best of luck, Bobby," she said. He realized he had never caught her name as she spoke. "And thank you for telling me your story." Then she got up and walked away. Bobby felt unsettled as he watched her abruptly leave. He sat alone on the bench, vulnerable and alone, the emotional aftermath settling like a dense fog.

He stood up and walked back into the waiting room, now stoic. He had cried enough. Now he just sat and waited. A little while later the family came back down and William gave Bobby the news. Willie was being kept alive on life support, and the doctors were going to spend the night trying to make sure there was nothing they could do.

"I am going to stay here tonight and wait; you are welcome to stay here with me," William said, and Bobby nodded in agreement.

William took out a chess set that the hospital had in their waiting room and asked Bobby if he would like to play. The two of them played chess all night, painfully eating up the longest night of either of their lives.

The next morning, on their seventh game of chess, Bobby was just about to take William's bishop when the doctor entered the waiting room.

"I'm sorry," the doctor said with a grave expression. "We tried everything we could."

The doctor continued but Bobby didn't listen, he had heard enough. Little Willie was dead. He suddenly felt the need to get away, to escape the eyes of the family he was sure stared at him with a judgmental rage. It had been his fault, hadn't it? The whole night prior William had tried to convince Bobby of the opposite.

"You did all you could, son," William had said.

Maybe I did, maybe I didn't. Bobby thought to himself. Either way, Little Willie was now dead, and there was nothing that could be done about that. Bobby stumbled out of the waiting room and into a long empty hallway.

The moment when Willie's head had dropped lifelessly as Bobby pulled him out of the water ran over and over again in Bobby's mind. Along the side of the hallway was an elevator door and in a sudden moment of rage Bobby threw himself against the metal elevator doors. He pounded his fists against the doors until his knuckles began to bleed and his strength ran out. Bobby then sank to his knees in defeat. For a while Bobby didn't move, but just knelt staring into his own distorted reflection through the now dented metal doors. Then in the reflection Bobby saw someone walk up behind him. William knelt down next to Bobby and put a comforting arm around him.

"Today I lost Little Willie," he said with a deep ring of sorrow in his voice. "Bobby, I don't want to lose you too."

Bobby was surprised by this man's compassion. William had just lost his son and was now reaching out to the very individual that was probably responsible for his son's death. Bobby did not respond; he was exhausted and could no longer even understand, much less articulate, what he was feeling. So Bobby got up, apologized one last time to William, and then walked out of the hospital.

As Bobby left the hospital and headed back to his house, he walked by a newsstand; on the front page of the *Kansas City Star* the headline read, "Inner City Lifeguard Lets Little Boy Drown."

The headline hit Bobby like a ton of bricks. His mind reeled as he picked up the paper and tore it open to the article. The author spoke of Bobby by name, about how he didn't know how to perform CPR, about how the city had hired a negligent lifeguard and never properly trained him. Bobby already felt responsible, but it was an entirely different thing to see the front page of the *Star* scream his failure.

Many of the accusations were actually said to be direct quotes from Bobby himself. How did they get all this information? Bobby thought to himself. And then he remembered the woman in the olive skirt. She was a reporter; she had only approached him when she smelled a story that had enough drama in it to reach the front page. She didn't care about him—she just wanted the juicy story. Even though he had hardly known the woman, he felt as if he had been betrayed by one of his closest friends.

Bobby tossed the paper into the nearest trash can and continued to walk back home. A mixture of anger and guilt stirred wildly inside of Bobby—but most of all, he felt terribly, terribly alone.

12

THE DEPOSITION

Later that same day, Bobby was contacted by the city. He was informed that Willie's mother had filed a wrongful death lawsuit against the city, and they needed Bobby to come in to the local court house for a deposition the next day. The mother was claiming the city should have hired properly trained lifeguards to prevent such disasters. The entire assumption was based upon a fear that was already looming in Bobby's mind: perhaps if he had gotten there faster, perhaps if he had not hesitated, perhaps if he had known CPR, then maybe Willie's life could've been saved. The thought of both struggling internally with his guilt and externally sorting out the facts with a group of lawyers was overwhelming.

Without anything to do or any way to preoccupy his mind, Bobby left to go find a bar. Although only seventeen, he could usually pass for older and make his way in. But on this particular afternoon, the bartender asked for Bobby's ID. Bobby pretended he had left it at home.

"Forget it, kid," the bartender responded.

"Come on. You don't know the day I have had," Bobby replied, losing his act.

"I don't care. Get lost," the bartender said, sounding surprisingly impatient.

Bobby was actually a bit excited when he heard the bartender's reaction. *Yeah, I've gotten into fights about less,* he thought to himself as he tightened his fists. Getting into a wild bar fight sounded oddly therapeutic, and he now had an opportunity. But before Bobby could throw his first punch, someone came up from behind him and interrupted the two.

"Hey Dave, this is Bobby Hartley! You can't deny service to Bobby Hartley," the voice from behind him said to the bartender.

Bobby turned to see an old friend from Saint Catherine's Gardens, Tim Deeter.

"You know this kid?" the bartender asked Tim.

"Of course, Bobby and I are old pals," Tim said as he slapped Bobby on the back.

That's a bit of an overstatement, Bobby thought to himself. Tim was about five years older than Bobby and had only befriended him because he wanted Bobby to peddle drugs for him. Tim was a marijuana dealer, and during Bobby's last few years in high school, Tim had approached Bobby several times about being a "salesman" for him. Bobby had never been interested in drugs, much less in selling them, so he refused. But Tim was convinced that Bobby had what it took to be a good salesman so he kept asking.

Even though Bobby didn't really consider Tim a friend, he still enjoyed Tim's company. And after some small talk and a couple of beers, Bobby ended up telling Tim the whole story about Willie, the newspaper article, and the lawsuit.

"Bobby," Tim said, shaking his head after Bobby finished his story. "I don't know what to say, man. That's the worst thing I've ever heard."

Both just sat silently for a few moments.

"You know if, uh, well, I don't want to sound like I'm trying to sell you at a time like this. But if you need something to take the edge off, you know I'm your man," Tim said with a genuine sense of empathy.

"I don't do drugs, Tim," Bobby said firmly. The answer was more automatic than it was heartfelt; right now he truly didn't care.

"Okay, well, if you need a job—I mean, you need keep yourself busy, man, and I'd keep a guy as talented as you real busy," Tim said.

"What do you mean, talented?" Bobby thought the idea was ridiculous.

"You're a likeable guy, Bobby, and you know how to work people. Plus you are a sharp kid, which is more than I can say about most of the guys I have working for me," Tim said with a scoff.

Bobby nodded his head and then stood up to head back home. "I'll think about it."

"My man! Just know it's a great job with great benefits—and money. Which, speaking of, I've got your drinks tonight." Tim turned to the bartender. "Put him on my tab, Dave."

"Thanks," Bobby said simply and headed home for the night.

When Bobby woke up the next morning, he had several hours to kill before the deposition, so he decided to go back to the pool to work. As much as he hated the thought of seeing the pool again, he hated the thought of being alone with nothing to do even more. But when he got there, the pool was closed. The city couldn't afford to keep it open while they were fighting the wrongful death suit. The pool was completely empty of everyone except Hughes and Yvette, who were covering the pool and stacking chairs.

Feeling numb, Bobby asked Hughes if there was anything he could do to help. Hughes nodded and asked if Bobby would go to the gas station a couple blocks away to pick up some things.

Yvette offered to come with for company. Yvette had only slowly began to tolerate Bobby; the way Bobby acted, toleration was often the highest he could hope for. But now, after Willie's death, Yvette saw the pain and hurt in Bobby's eyes and was overwhelmed with a strong sense of compassion. The two walked to the gas station, neither saying much, but just before they arrived, Yvette stopped Bobby.

"It's going to be okay," she said confidently.

Bobby wondered how many times she had looked at herself in the mirror and said those exact words. When she spoke, Bobby knew it was coming from experience, not speculation.

But his moment of comfort quickly dissipated. The clerk at the gas station had the *Kansas City Star* in hand and was conversing with a customer about the "the lifeguard who let the little boy drown." Apparently Willie's death and the law suit had become a conversation point in the city. The clerk spoke of Bobby's negligence and ineptitude, although he expressed his feelings with a few choice four-letter words that he obviously felt more comfortable with than "negligence" or "ineptitude."

Bobby listened in silence. He had always been able to dismiss negative comments and opinions. He truly didn't care about others' perceptions of him; he learned at an early age that people's opinions were fickle and trying to please everyone was far too complex of a task.

But at this moment, Bobby had no idea who he was. He couldn't care less what the clerk's perception of him was, but the words that the clerk spoke gave a voice to the fears and accusations that had begun to echo in Bobby's own head. Each off-handed judgmental comment stabbed. The clerk, however, evoked quite a different emotion from Yvette. Infuriated by his insensitivity, Yvette began to boil, and finally she snapped. She reached over the counter and picked the clerk up by his shirt.

"That lifeguard has a name and it is Bobby Hartley!" Yvette yelled as she shook the clerk, whose face twisted in both terror and confusion. "And Bobby Hartley is a fine young man who did all he could to help that little boy." She had pulled so hard on the clerk and brought him so close to her face that most of his body was now hanging over the counter. Yvette suddenly let him go, and the clerk dropped head first to the ground and rolled into a shelf, sending magazines and candy bars spilling across the floor. Yvette picked up one of the magazines and began to slap the clerk with it.

"Say you're sorry!" she yelled.

"Okay, I'm sorry!" he whimpered.

Yvette dropped the magazine, stormed out the front door, and headed back to the pool. Bobby, with a subtle smile, followed close behind.

That afternoon Bobby made his way to city hall where he was told to go to the thirteenth floor for his deposition. Bobby was decorously led to a seat at a long table along with over a dozen city lawyers. As soon as Bobby sat down, a lawyer, who had introduced himself as Mr. Wilcox, catapulted into instructions.

"Alright Mr. Hartley, I'm going to explain something to you very briefly before we jump in here." His tone was loud and spiteful. "You're in all sorts of trouble. You messed up big time and the whole city knows about it."

Bobby was taken aback by Mr. Wilcox's harshness, but as he looked around at the blank faces, he couldn't help but internally scoff their pretentiousness.

"Now we can help you Mr. Hartley. We can maybe get you out of this. But you need to do everything we say. No questions asked. Do you hear me?"

Bobby didn't respond but just folded his arms and leaned back in his chair.

"Mr. Hartley, do you hear me?" Mr. Wilcox repeated.

Bobby nodded slowly. "Yeah, I hear you."

"Okay, good. Now this is what you are going to do. You are not going to talk to anyone, besides us, about what happened. Not the press, not other lawyers, not your friends, I don't care if your own mother calls to check up on you. You don't talk with anyone besides us. Okay?" Without pausing, Mr. Wilcox continued. "We are flying in the world's best water safety instructor, and tomorrow you are going to train with him. You will do absolutely everything the instructor tells you and in three weeks, before the trial, you are going to become the best lifeguard in this state. Is that clear?"

Mr. Wilcox was not messing around. This lawsuit could possibly expose liability worth millions of dollars against the city, and Bobby's testimony was one of the most important aspects of the case. Mr. Wilcox was intimidating and imposing, and especially considering the exposure Bobby had just experienced, he figured Bobby would melt before him. He had figured wrong.

"Clear? I'll tell you what's clear to me," Bobby defiantly responded. "It's clear what you want me to do; you want me just to roll over and play dead. You want me to be your little puppet so you can cover yourself and make sure the city gets off free. But let me make something clear to you, Mr. Wilcox. This is what I'm actually going to do. I'm going to stand up for myself, and I'm not going to let a [jerk] like you walk all over me."

Bobby paused for a moment to let his point settle.

"And as for the water safety instructor—well, the water is just about the last place I want to be right now so I think I might just decline," Bobby stated matter-of-factly.

Bobby had never taken very kindly to bullies or men in thousand-dollar suits, and as he looked around the table, he noted how often those two things coincided.

"You think we are tough, Mr. Hartley? You just wait until you are in court and the plaintiff's attorney starts in on you. I don't think you realize that you are the primary witness. Whatever they say about the city is secondary to what they say about you. They will destroy your identity and make you into a monster so that they can sue the city for hiring you. They will ruin your public image." Mr. Wilcox stated with an unsettling composure.

"You can't break something that's already broken," Bobby said, still not moved. "I don't care what others think about me."

"Do you ever want to go to college, Mr. Hartley?" Mr. Wilcox asked rhetorically, but Bobby responded anyway.

"No, not really."

"Well how about any future at all? Good luck getting a job anywhere in this city," Mr. Wilcox continued.

"Oddly enough, I just got a great job offer yesterday. Good pay, good benefits, too," Bobby said. "And don't pretend like you actually care about me, this is all just about protecting the city," Bobby continued.

"A sentiment I would expect you to care more about, considering your father himself is employed by the city." Mr. Wilcox said.

Bobby was thrown off-balance.

"What are you saying?"

"I am just saying you shouldn't be quick to bite the hand that feeds you," Mr. Wilcox said in a tone that made Bobby's skin crawl.

"That sounds like a threat," Bobby said, expecting an immediate response. Instead, he got a cold stare.

"Okay, well," Bobby said as he stood from his seat and looked to the other lawyers. "I'm done." And with that Bobby turned and began to walk out.

"Hang on, Mr. Hartley, we still need to hear what happened." Mr. Wilcox said forcefully.

"Read a newspaper," Bobby said without looking back, and he walked out the door.

That night Bobby returned home from another night of drinking to find several messages on his answering machine. Most of them were from newspaper reporters and lawyers. One message was from Mr. Wilcox reminding Bobby to go to the Oak Grove county pool for the water safety instructor at ten the next morning. Bobby wrote down the information, but he was still unconvinced. The last message on the machine was from Tim Deeter.

"Hey Bobby, just wondering how you're handling everything, man, and I was wondering if you had thought more about my offer. Anyway, let me know."

For years Bobby had avoided drugs and the lifestyle that went with it, but there was something always enticing about that world. He wondered what had kept him from accepting Tim's many offers. Well, whatever it was no longer existed; any shred of moral dignity Bobby once had was now gone.

He picked up the phone and dialed the number Tim had left him.

"Okay, I'm in," he said.

13

INSTRUCTED

It took Bobby a full night to decide whether he was going to attend the water safety instruction class. He desperately wanted to skip out. Mr. Wilcox and the rest of the lawyers had swarmed Bobby, hawking like a group of vultures picking clean the remains of a dying animal. Acquiescing to their plan was the last thing he wanted to do. But then again, he didn't have a whole lot of options. Mr. Wilcox's words had rattled Bobby. He hated to admit it to himself, but he was afraid. He knew if he wanted to survive this lawsuit, he couldn't really be out making enemies. Besides, if Bobby didn't show up, he knew they would see him as a quitter. And more than anything else, that's what ended up forcing his hand.

When Bobby first met the water safety instructor he nearly turned right around and headed straight home. The instructor, who had introduced himself as Joe, was an overweight man who did not exactly leave anyone with an impression of his athletic competence. *This man moves like a beached whale. How could he possibly train me?* Bobby thought. He leaned over to one of his co-workers. "How fitting it would be if the man teaching us how to save people has a heart attack in the middle of training. Hope he teaches us CPR first," Bobby whispered.

The whole staff of the pool had been called in to go through the course and only about half of Bobby's coworkers had shown up. But it didn't really matter; the whole thing was set up for Bobby. When Joe began to address the crew, his gaze was glued on Bobby.

"If you don't learn everything I teach you over the next few days, people will die, and it will be on your hands," Joe rattled out. He wore a cynical expression and spoke more like a boot camp drill sergeant than a water safety instructor.

Bobby was shocked by the man's insensitivity. Of course Joe knew all about what had happened with Little Willie, and here he was insinuating exactly what the *Kansas City Star* had concluded: it was Bobby's negligence that had resulted in Willie's death.

Bobby began to swell with anger as Joe continued to berate the employees for their inabilities.

"You are a bunch of kids who took a job without the slightest idea of what it required. So I'm here to show you what will be required of you from now on." As Joe spoke, the layer of fat that hung from his jaw jiggled from side to side.

"Many of you will find training too difficult. Over half of you will likely give up and quit. If you do, don't bother coming back to work. You should never have been hired in the first place." Joe had developed a rather loose tongue throughout the years and was now in the process of removing certain unprofessional words from his vocabulary—resulting in a sort of stutter as he would pause between occasional words to censor himself. "Now let's start. Which one of you kids wants to volunteer to show me how they would pull someone out of the water?"

No one raised their hand.

"Well how about we start with you," Joe said as he pointed at Bobby.

Of course, Bobby thought to himself.

Joe hopped into the water and waded out into the middle of the pool.

"Alright, now I want you to jump in and pull me out of the water," Joe said as Bobby looked on incredulously. Joe was not a small man, and pulling him out of the water would be no small task.

"Come on! Don't hesitate. You are losing precious seconds."

Bobby released a sigh, lazily hopped into the pool, and swam over to Joe.

"A drowning victim will instinctively fight you, pushing you down in order to get themselves closer to the surface," Joe instructed as Bobby began to reach underneath Joe's arms to hook him and pull him back to the side of the pool. Joe grabbed Bobby and shoved him underneath the water. Bobby struggled, but with his massive arms Joe easily kept Bobby restrained and completely submerged.

The rest of the staff looked on, stunned, as Joe continued to hold Bobby underneath the water for what seemed like too long. Joe talked to the class as he wrestled Bobby down, "See this is why if you do not know the proper way to approach someone in the water, they could—" Joe stopped mid-sentence and let out a painful yelp.

Fueled by anger and desperation, Bobby sunk his teeth into Joe's forearm, startling him into loosening his grip. Bobby popped up to the surface and pushed himself behind Joe. Bobby had learned in wrestling that wherever the head goes, the body follows, so he yanked on Joe's chin, pulling his head forcefully toward the side of the pool. When they got close enough to the side, rather than trying to pull Joe out of the pool, Bobby just turned and pushed Joe into the cement wall.

Joe slammed face first against the wall. His lip split open and blood to start spilling out. Bobby swam back to the center of the pool.

"Come on!" Bobby exclaimed. "Let's go again!"

For the next few days, Bobby attended the water safety course, and as each day passed the training got progressively harder. Joe would have Bobby and the rest of the staff swim dozens of laps back and forth while fully clothed. If any of them touched the bottom or held the side wall they all had to start over. He would make them tread water while holding weights above their heads. Each day, the weights would get heavier and the number of laps would increase. On the second day, only a handful of the staff showed up. On the third day, even fewer showed up. And by the time the fourth day rolled around every single staff member had quit; everyone that is, except for Bobby.

The city needed Bobby to be humble, they needed him to be coachable, but most of all, they needed him to be moldable. When the court date rolled around they couldn't have a loose cannon on their hands. They needed someone they could control. Joe was there to do more than just train Bobby on water safety; he was there to iron out Bobby's obdurate wrinkles.

"Forget it. I'm done," Bobby told Joe firmly as he pulled himself out of the water after a grueling workout the fourth and final day. It was well past their scheduled class time, and Bobby had finally reached his limit.

"You'll be finished when I say so," Joe responded as he stepped in front of the gate blocking Bobby's exit.

"You know, I'm sick of this. I've proven I am, and have always been, more than capable for this job." Bobby said as he began to lose his cool. "Now, get out of my way."

For a moment Joe stood there, motionless. But then, without a word, he stepped to the side. Bobby was already halfway through the parking lot before Joe spoke. "Bobby, wait," he pleaded. Bobby paused but did not look back. "Don't give up. Come back tomorrow and I promise it will be the last day."

Bobby was surprised by the change of tone in Joe's voice. Regardless, Bobby wasn't interested. He walked on without responding.

The next day Bobby woke up to Joe knocking at his door.

"I'm not coming." Bobby said simply, and then went to shut the door, but Joe shoved his foot inside.

"Hang on. I didn't come here to make you come to training. I just came here to talk," Joe said with an uncharacteristically soft voice.

"You have ten minutes. Then I need to get to work," Bobby said with a sigh as he opened the door.

The work Bobby was referring to was his first real drug deal. Tim had introduced Bobby to a few local marijuana suppliers, and Bobby had bought a fairly sizable quantity and was planning on redistributing it to a group of customers made up of old high school friends and a couple of names Tim had given Bobby to "help him hit the ground running."

Joe walked in and glanced around Bobby's house, completely perplexed by what he saw. Bobby had been renting the house for the last four months from a private owner. The owner never came by as long as the rent was in on time, so Bobby had taken a few artistic liberties with his decorating. He had taken all of the expensive furniture in the house and sold it for top dollar at local furniture stores and pawn shops. He replaced them with couches, desks, and chairs he found in dumpsters or at garage sales across the city. None of it matched and most of it was falling apart. But Bobby didn't care; he had collected enough money in the exchange to pay for almost a full six months' worth of rent.

As Joe glanced around he was confounded. The place was a dump, yet it was a somewhat orderly and decently maintained dump. The couch looked as if it had been salvaged from the wreckage of a burned down building. Several kitchen knives stuck firmly in the living room drywall; Bobby had painted a bull's eye five feet off the ground and used it for knife throwing target practice. The light bulbs in the ceiling had been replaced with black lights and a broken disco ball hung from the ceiling fan. Yet, the carpet was vacuumed, there was a scented candle lit on the kitchen table, and in the entrance there was a welcome mat that read "Please remove your shoes." A picture in the family room read "Cleanliness is Next to Godliness," and Joe wondered whether it was hung with irony or sincerity.

"So, what do you want?" Bobby asked with a measure of both impatience and curiosity.

Joe stopped evaluating the room and turned his attention back to Bobby.

"Do you want to know why I became a swim instructor?"

Bobby shrugged.

Joe continued, taking Bobby's indifference as a yes.

"When I was eighteen years old, not that much older then you are now, I went to the lake with my little brother. We had made a little raft out of wood, and we thought it would be fun to take it out. So we paddled out, convinced we could cross the whole lake. It was a crappy little thing and to be honest I don't know how we got anywhere on it." Joe flashed a subtle smile but it disappeared almost instantly as he continued his story. "We made it all the way out into to the middle of the lake before it broke apart. Neither of us were very good swimmers, so we panicked and swam as fast as we could toward the shore. It wasn't long before my brother started sinking down. I mean we still had all of our clothes on and everything. I tried to pull him along, but I was worried I wasn't going to make it myself. So I left him. I left my little brother drowning in the middle of the lake because I had no idea how to save him. I thought maybe if I got to the shore quickly enough I could find help, but—" Joe shook his head and paused, lost in the swirl of memories and emotions. "I got to the shore and found somebody with a boat, but of course by the time we got back out there it was way too late. He was nine." For a few moments Joe just sat there as the weight of the story washed over Bobby. "How old was he? The boy you pulled out of the pool, how old was he?"

"Six," Bobby responded quietly.

"Such a shame," Joe replied. Then after a heavy pause, "Look, I know you think that I don't care about you and that I don't have any idea what you're going through. And to be honest, I don't blame you. I've been tough on you, I know that. But I do care. And I do know exactly what you're going through."

"Normally the good cop/bad cop approach works best with two people," Bobby said with a scoff.

"Well, maybe I've been too tough. But look, you can't do this alone, Bobby. You're a tough kid, and you're one of the best lifeguards I've ever trained. I know you can make it through this lawsuit, you just...you can't do it all on your own. That's all I was trying to get you to realize."

Bobby stood up and walked to the door. "Alright, time's up."

Joe nodded as he stood up. "Yeah, okay. Thanks for letting me in." Bobby opened the door and let Joe out. After he took several steps outside, Joe turned around. "You know, you're not alone, Bobby." And with that, Joe turned, got in his car, and drove away.

Bobby walked back into his living room and sat down on his couch. He eyed an expensive painting that hung from the wall across from the couch. He had stolen the painting about three weeks ago. It had become a bit of a habit. He would sneak into art galleries or hotel lobbies and steal their paintings. Not for the love of art—Bobby couldn't distinguish the high-brow stuff from elementary school doodles. He did it just for the thrill. He would steal the paintings, then take them back to his house and throw knives at them.

But this painting was different. It was of a boy and his father walking down a dock to fish. He didn't know why, but for some reason he actually liked this painting. He would probably throw knives at it later, but for now, he just looked at it.

14

THE RAMADA INN

Bobby flipped through the pages of the *Kansas City Star* as he sat behind the Ramada Inn check-in desk. He had taken the job a couple of months before to fill some extra hours. Each week Bobby had asked for more hours, and each week his request was granted. What started out as a part time job had quickly become a full time job; now he was spending almost every night at the hotel. Bobby had just about finished his shift when they brought in the *Star*'s morning print—so he quickly nabbed one and began to anxiously skim through it: an advertisement for Marlboro pictured a cowboy smoking as he cooked over a fire, a lengthy article about a flu shot scare in New York, obituaries, horoscopes, and comics—not a single word about the lawsuit against the city for employing a negligent lifeguard.

After a full two years of procedural posturing and scrutiny, the court had concluded that Willie's death was not caused by the negligence of Bobby or the city. The *Star* had plastered it all over town when the lawsuit was first brought but didn't find the lawsuit's conclusion newsworthy. Bobby folded up the newspaper and tossed it into the garbage can. It bothered him for a second, but it didn't stick with him long. He was just happy to be done with it all. Throughout those two years, settlement negotiations had forced Bobby to rehash the event over and over again. Maybe it was a good thing that the *Star* didn't print anything; the public had seemingly forgotten about it. The past was burying itself. It was time to move on to the future, which, to Bobby, seemed increasingly rosy. He enjoyed his life and had a newfound sense of self-respect and confidence, primarily due to his success as a drug dealer.

Bobby was a natural at drug dealing. Motivated and charismatic, he had a dwindling set of moral standards and a complete disregard for ethical, legal, or physical consequences. Bobby's salesmanship set him apart from his competitors; his knack for business and his commitment to the ordering of his accounts, the structuring of his sales, and the distribution of the product made him one of the most profitable dealers in Kansas City. In many ways, his life improved the more he became integrated with the drug scene. Dealing produced a steady income and gave him limitless opportunities for expansion. And more than the money, Bobby needed the work. It was cathartic. He craved busyness and responsibility—it kept him focused, it stretched him, and most importantly, it kept him preoccupied. The pain of his life and past failures, specifically the death of Little Willie, had no time to grip Bobby as long as he kept moving. If a rolling stone gathers no moss, then Bobby was a boulder in free fall.

Even though he was selling drugs immoderately, Bobby used the drugs very selectively. He didn't like the mind-altering state that many of the drugs put him into because they sapped his drive and motivation. He didn't want to escape the world; he wanted to conquer it. The only drug Bobby began to use on a regular basis was actually a legal drug often called trucker speed, ephedrine tablets sold at gas stations under the name "mini thins" and designed as a recreational stimulant and energy booster. "Truckers" were cheaper and not nearly as damaging as most of Bobby's inventory, but due to Bobby's intense schedule, he began using truckers on a daily basis and started developing a dependency. Bobby arranged his schedule tightly, giving himself little time for sleep, so he would mix truckers with incredible amounts of caffeine. He began to wreck his sleep schedule, often going days without sleeping, and getting, on average, only two hours of sleep a night.

While the stress and adrenaline of drug dealing kept him awake and active, he would often find himself dozing off while doing the mundane activities required of him by the Ramada Inn. Just earlier that day, when vacuuming the hallways, Bobby had fallen asleep standing up. He just stood there, head tilted back, vacuum whirring loudly, in the middle of the hallway, until his own snoring woke him up.

Bobby glanced down at his watch and calculated just how long he had left before he could go home and get some sleep. 5:38 A.M., less than a half hour to go. He sighed and rested his head on the desk. A short nap wouldn't hurt anybody.

"Bobby!"

The shout broke the serene silence and startled Bobby back to consciousness. He jolted up to see one of his coworkers, Randy, pointing furiously toward the business center.

"Quick, get him! He's here! He's taking our paper!"

At first Bobby just stared at Randy, confused. But then he remembered: for the past couple of months a kid had been coming into the business center in the lobby of the Ramada Inn and stealing reams of copy paper. *What type of crazy would steal paper from a hotel?* Bobby thought, and ran down the hall to pursue the crook. Bobby had just turned the corner to the business center when he saw a lanky redhead bust through the back door with a stack of paper in his hand. Bobby took off in pursuit. A trail of papers flitted through the air as the boy bounded across the parking lot. Bobby began gaining ground and thought he had the boy cornered when the parking lot had run out and only a large fence stood in front of them. To Bobby's surprise, the boy didn't hesitate but leapt over the fence in a single bound.

Not about to let the culprit escape, Bobby flung himself head first over the fence, front flipped over it, then landed on his shoulder and rolled forward onto his feet. But Bobby suddenly came to a stop. The boy had turned and was now standing directly over him. He had dropped his papers and was in a quasi-karate stance breathing steadily while he stared at Bobby intensely.

"I'm sorry, but it looks like I'm going to have to kill you," the boy breathed with a crazed look in his eye as he held his Karate Kid/praying mantis stance. He was pencil-thin and looked to be just about as threatening as Steve Urkel. Bobby stood up slowly, unfazed by the ridiculous threat but sensing something familiar in the kid's voice. Bobby knew he recognized it. He squinted to see if he could make out the face in the dim light.

"Billy Algile?" Bobby asked, recognizing his childhood friend who had collected rotten bananas and thrown them at the school bus every day.

"Billy, it's me! Bobby Hartley!"

Billy took a moment to look at Bobby and then nodded with recognition.

"Sorry Bobby—I still have to kill you," Billy said as he once again recoiled into his awkward pounce position.

"Oh shut up, Billy," Bobby said as he straightened and brushed himself off. "Grab your paper and get out of here. I'll tell them you got away."

Billy immediately grabbed the stack of paper and scampered off into the woods.

15

THE KID WITH THE COKE BOTTLE GLASSES

The kid with the Coke bottle glasses sat placidly in the back corner of the Bobby's house smoking a cigarette as he watched Bobby and his team go about their business: a couple of guys in the back cleaning and removing the stocks from the marijuana, a couple more up front weighing it and bagging it, and another collecting the exchanged money and keeping it safe. All the while Bobby was supervising, making sure everything ran smoothly. Everyone had defined roles on the team so they could operate with efficiency, but also so that if they were ever caught, they could only be tried for one thing. Bobby had started opening up his house for his customers to come and go as they like; he found business was better when his customers felt comfortable. Often the customers would bring their friends and hang out for a bit, and subsequently, Bobby's sales had grown exponentially. But it also meant a good number of odd and wayward individuals would find their way into Bobby's house. And this kid with the Coke bottle glasses—well, Bobby wasn't quite sure what to make of him. He had slipped in with a group of regulars; Bobby had assumed he was a friend of theirs. But when the regulars all left and this kid stayed, Bobby started feeling uneasy.

Earlier that month, there had been a major drug bust involving one of Bobby's suppliers in downtown Kansas City and the word on the street was that the police had acquired the supplier's "distribution list." Most suppliers would keep a detailed list of all of their trustworthy distributers so they could make sure they weren't dealing with anyone who could be an undercover cop. Bobby was certain that his name was on this list, so for the past few months he had been looking over his shoulder in a perpetual state of fear.

The kid took a long, patient drag of his cigarette. His hair slicked down to his shoulders, tangling itself in a greasy unkempt mess. His eyes were hidden behind his thick, dark glasses that rested on a long crooked nose. He hadn't said a word since he had arrived, hadn't purchased anything; he just sat in a side chair and watched. Bobby had thought about kicking the kid out, but odd behavior like the kid was displaying was by no means uncommon and Bobby just told himself that he was being overly suspicious. For two hours, the kid sat in the corner watching dozens of exchanges as dozens of customers came in and out. Finally, at the end of the night, he got up and pulled his chair uncomfortably close to Bobby as he sat counting the daily earnings.

"You have a fine operation going on here, Bobby," the kid said as he pulled out a new cigarette from his pocket.

"Do I know you?" Bobby responded, a bit confused about how this kid knew his name.

"My name is Charlie. Charlie Chism." He paused for a moment to light the cigarette. "Bobby, I would like to tell you a story."

For the next hour Charlie told Bobby, in explicit detail, how he himself had been a drug dealer. His story was so similar to Bobby's, it was both comforting and haunting. It was like traveling in a foreign country and suddenly meeting someone who not only speaks your language, but also grew up in your hometown. Yet the similarities also felt uncanny. Even though Charlie looked no older then eighteen or nineteen years old, he was actually twenty-five and had spent the last two years in prison. He told Bobby how he had gotten too cocky and started selling too much. He wouldn't discriminate or filter his customers; he just invited anybody in.

"I thought I was untouchable. I became careless, reckless. And for that reason alone, I deserved to go to prison."

Charlie then went on to tell exactly how he got busted. How one day someone came to his house where he was making the drug deals, watched him for several hours, then left. He later found out the person was a police informant and had reported everything, every step of the operation, every deal that went down, all to the police. A month later, Charlie was arrested for drug dealing.

It was a clear and obvious correlation and Bobby immediately vocalized his fears. "So, how do I know you're not here to do the same thing to me?" Bobby asked.

"You don't." Charlie said, then he stood up, put out his cigarette, and walked outside.

For weeks, Bobby's conversation with Charlie haunted him. Why had Charlie told him all of that? If he was an informant, why warn Bobby? Was he just trying to scare Bobby?

Bobby had no idea what to do—it's not like he could just stop. There were dozens of individuals who relied on Bobby and who would not considerately walk away if they showed up and he had nothing to sell. Plus this was his life, he couldn't just up and quit. So Bobby continued to live in paranoia, just waiting for something to happen.

In the middle of the night about three weeks after his conversation with Charlie, Bobby woke up in a cold sweat. An unnatural fear gripped him; he didn't know why, but he knew he needed to get out of his house. Immediately, Bobby pushed up his window and jumped out.

He looked around expecting to see the police preparing to raid his house or a rival drug dealer with ill-intentions, but the street was empty. He hid across the street for several minutes just waiting and watching. After about fifteen minutes, he got up to go back in his house. *Maybe it was just a bad nightmare,* he thought to himself. He tried to slow his heart rate and convince himself he could go back inside. But then, the light in his bedroom flipped on. A cold chill ran down his spine. He hadn't seen anyone go in and there was no one else who lived in the house besides him.

He spent the next few hours walking around his house keeping a safe distance away. Eventually the light went off, yet he didn't see anyone come out. He waited for another thirty minutes and then went back into his house to find it had been ransacked. The house was completely trashed; his drawers, his cabinets, and his bed had all been ripped apart. They had even torn the posters off of his wall trying to find anything behind them.

He had no idea whether they were the police, a rival drug dealer, or maybe just a random robbery. But what was the most perplexing was how he had known it was coming. *How did I know to get out?* he thought as he collected a few essentials from the mess.

He needed to find a different place to stay and needed to figure out how to get out of town. He had no idea who had come in and ransacked his place, but he did not want to be around when they came back.

16

JUST TEACHER AND STUDENT

"Mr. Hartley, how are you doing today?" Ben, the local mailman, cheerily asked as he stepped through the door that wore a bronze plaque engraved with "Principal Hartley."

"Doing just fine, Ben, thank you," John Hartley responded with a genuine smile.

"Well, here's your mail," Ben said, handing it over. Ben had now been delivering the mail to John for over six years, always coming in to deliver the mail personally instead of simply dropping it off in the school's mailbox. John always enjoyed Ben's bright and conversational visits. But over the past year, John had noticed that Ben was becoming less and less talkative and hardly ever stopped to have a real conversation anymore. When he asked about it, Ben simply responded with a sharp smile, "Well, honestly I'm moving a bit slower these days... been a lot more like the tortoise than the hare as of late. Don't want to linger too long or else I'll get fired before I work up the guts to quit."

Age was beginning to take its toll on Ben's body, and he was no longer able to move at the same pace as he used to. But no matter how much of a rush he was ever in, Ben always found the time to ask John one question.

"How is your wife doing?"

He had asked it every single day since the surgery that left Ann bedridden.

Ann's doctors had speculated that after several years her body would begin to recover from the accident, and her pain would start to subside. But it had been almost six years, and her condition had not yet improved, making it very hard for either her or John to hold onto hope.

"Getting better," John said with a nod, and then repeated slowly, "Getting better."

"Well, that's good to hear. You know I'll be praying for her."

"Thank you, Ben."

Ben nodded and started to walk out but then turned back around as he recalled something.

"Oh Mr. Hartley, I just want to let you know, I've decided to retire at the end of this quarter," he said, beaming with a sense of self accomplishment. "I told my boss and got it all figured out. And you know, I think it's about time."

"Well, you sure deserve it. But I have to say I'm surprised; I figured you would be working until they had to fire you or carry you out in a casket," John joked.

"Yeah, you know, I thought that, too. I guess even an old guy like me can still surprise himself." Ben said with a nod, looking at his watch as he turned and headed back out the door. "But I best be going, wouldn't it just be like my boss to fire me a few months before I retired?"

"I guess you'll just have to hop the fence today—that'll make up the time."

A four foot high fence stretched the school property and only had one gate, located at the front of the school. Each day, Ben had to walk several hundred yards to the gate and then around the corner to his next stop on his route. He had once remarked how he had been a hurdler in college and probably still had the strength in him to hop the fence. Nearly every day since, then the two joked about how one day Ben was going to finally jump the fence. Even though John knew it was a joke, he would still glance out of his office window as Ben walked around the fence, just in case he ever decided to jump it.

The next day, John got up early and headed to Longview, a local community college, for his first day of teaching for the new school year. Along with his job as a principal, John had begun to teach weekend classes at a few different local colleges. They were the highlight of his week. As he opened the classroom door and stepped into the bustle of new students introducing themselves to one another, he couldn't help but feel a great sense of excitement and anticipation for the new year.

The class was large, and he wondered how long it would take to learn all of the names and faces. He glanced over the group quickly and then turned his back to them to write on the chalkboard. To open the class, John had decided to write one of his favorite quotes, a quote he had used in his own life many times.

"Good morning class, I'm Mr. Hartley. And today we will begin the school year with a quote by the great playwright, Oscar Wilde," John said as he scribbled the quote up on the board. Halfway through writing the quote he began to read it aloud to the class.

"'Education is an admirable thing, but it is well to remember from time to time that—'" Before John could finish writing, a voice in the back interrupted him and finished the phrase.

"'—nothing that is worth knowing can be taught.'"

John set down the chalk and turned to face the class. He recognized that voice.

"Bobby," John said as his eyes met those of his son, the son he had not seen nor heard from in over three years. "It's good to see you."

At first, John could hardly even recognize his Bobby. He was a disheveled mess, long mangy hair, dirty clothes, and years of sleepless nights worn onto a thinned face. But John still couldn't help but beam with affection as he looked upon his son.

"It's good to see you too, Dad," Bobby responded, causing the whole class to stare in amazement as they watched the reunion of a loving father and his wayward son.

"You know your mother really misses you."

"Okay Dad," Bobby responded simply.

"Well, it would be great to have you come visit sometime," John said, not quite sure what more to say. Bobby did not respond to John's invitation, but just nodded. For a few seconds John stood silently, and then he turned and went on to teach the class.

17

THANKSGIVING

After his house had been ransacked, Bobby enrolled into a couple of intensive weekend classes at Longview College in order to boost his transcripts so he had a better chance of getting into a state college. His hope was to attend Central Missouri State University in the winter so that he could get out of town before he was picked up and sent to jail for drug dealing. When he enrolled, he had no idea his dad would be teaching his first class. In fact, he didn't even know his dad had begun teaching at the college until he walked into the classroom.

For the next few months neither Bobby nor John knew quite how to interact with one another. John loved his son and wanted to reconnect and hear about Bobby's life. He also wanted to give Bobby space. It was not like John to force his way into anyone's life; he knew Bobby would invite him back in whenever he was ready. Beyond the occasional cordial hello, the two never really spoke.

As much as Bobby truly cared for his dad, he had no intention of mixing his old life with the present. Bobby was a little incredulous of who he had become and preferred not to subject himself to shame in addition to the past pains he did not wish to relive. So Bobby avoided his father, often not even showing up for class. Bobby knew John's curriculum so he would just get the assignments and study guides from a friend who was also in the class.

A week before Thanksgiving, well into the school year, Bobby showed up to class in order to take a scheduled test. After the class, Bobby headed straight for his car, but John stopped him before he had a chance to leave.

"Hey Bobby, I don't know if you have any plans already, but I would love it if you could come for Thanksgiving next week. The whole family wants to see you!" John invited.

"I don't know Dad," Bobby said hesitantly. "Maybe."

"Okay, well, just know the door is open." John wasn't going to push Bobby, but rather give him the opportunity. At the moment, Bobby didn't really even give the idea a chance. No way would he want to reenter that world.

The night before Thanksgiving, Bobby partied with his friends, not stopping until well into the early morning. Often before big family holidays, like Thanksgiving or Christmas, Bobby and his friends would party all night so that they could sleep through the day. They didn't want to be awake only to have nothing to do and nowhere to go. But as Bobby returned to his home that Thanksgiving morning, he couldn't fall asleep. He tossed in his bed for what seemed like hours. Something deep down inside of Bobby was eating away at him, urging him to go see his family.

The Hartley family always began Thanksgiving early, eating breakfast together, playing football, and watching the parades on TV—killing time until Thanksgiving dinner. After an hour of debating with himself, Bobby threw on a new shirt and left his house without getting any sleep, so as to make it in time for the Hartley's family breakfast. When he drove up to his parents' house, he sat in his car for several minutes questioning what he was actually doing. "What am I going to say?" He felt nervous and out of place. But he was already there; someone must have seen him park outside, so it was too late to back out. He took a few breaths, walked up to the door, and knocked. His grandmother answered the door and stared for a few moments at him.

"My, you used to be a cute boy," she said with a furrowed brow and a disapproving tone.

She was the type of woman who, if you said, "It's a nice day out" to her, she would respond, "Ah, well, it will rain tomorrow."

"It's good to see you, too, Nana," Bobby responded. She had always been cranky, and Bobby was long used to her disapproval. But even though he knew it was coming and knew it was warranted, her words still hurt.

Bobby exchanged hellos with the rest of his family. He looked around, feeling as if he didn't know any of them anymore. He did his best to jumpstart a conversation with a couple of his family members, trying desperately to simulate normalcy, but it just didn't seem to work.

The day dragged on, and the longer he stayed there, the more he felt overwhelmed with a powerful sense of guilt. When it was eventually time for dinner, Bobby was nearly in tears. He looked around the table at his family as everyone sat down, a family he had deserted. He had set off on his own, so sure that he could do more by himself without the rest of them weighing him down.

He caught a glimpse of his own reflection in a long mirror that stretched across the back wall of the kitchen.

Look at me, he thought to himself, *I'm a mess.* His hair had grown long and unmanageable and his eyes were dark from intense sleep deprivation. He could not believe what he had become, or more so, what he hadn't become. He was a drug dealer and a thief, possessing no vision for the future and doing his best to forget the past.

Suddenly Bobby could not stand to be at the table any longer. He shifted in his seat, trying desperately to force himself to sit still. But all he wanted to do was to leave, to be out of the sight of his family—a family he had rejected, wounded, and disappointed. It took everything within him to keep himself still and seated at the table. For what must have been several minutes Bobby didn't once look up from his plate. The table, as always in the Hartley household, was active and chaotic as dozens of individuals held separate conversations at the same time. So Bobby kept his head down in hopes he would just fade into the background.

Several of the family members began to speak of what they were most thankful for. There was no order or system to who spoke or who was next in line. Someone would just chime in, several people would interrupt and interject, and then suddenly someone else would start saying what they were thankful for as the other tried to finish. It eventually just descended into a chaotic mess of people talking about a hundred different things over one another. But that's the way any Hartley meal ever was, and that was the way they liked it.

When Bobby finally looked up, it startled him to see his father staring straight at him. With only love and appreciation in his eyes, John spoke:

"I'm proud of you, son."

John's words sent Bobby's world spinning. John was always a man who believed in people and had a hope for everyone he encountered. But he grew up in a time when such affirmation was rarely stated, especially from a father to his son. Bobby had always known his father cared for him, but to hear that his dad was proud of him, especially considering his messed-up situation, was dizzying.

"No, Dad, you don't know what I've done; you don't know where I've been," Bobby said as he shook his head.

"I know who you are, Bobby." The whole table had drawn silent as they listened to John speak. "I know you are going to pin your problems to the mat."

Tears formed and began to spill down Bobby's face as he tried his best to keep his composure.

"Bobby, you are going to be quite a man someday, and you are going to touch a lot of lives." John spoke with such a confidence it seemed as if it had already happened, as if there was not a doubt in his mind. And even though Bobby couldn't fathom the possibility, in that moment, he couldn't help but believe the words of his father.

A week later, John thought back on his conversation with his son as he organized some papers in his office. Bobby had left almost immediately after their conversation, and John really had no idea what had been going through Bobby's mind during that time. But really, when was he, or anyone else for that matter, able to know what was going through Bobby's head? John hoped that his words had stuck; he hoped that his words had meant something, but there was really no way to know for sure.

John's thoughts were interrupted by a welcome voice.

"How are you doing today, Mr. Hartley?" Ben said as he strolled into John's open door.

"Well Ben, I don't know; I guess I've been better," John said as he shook his head. "I just can't figure out what I am going to do without you."

Ben beamed his trademark smile; it was his last day before retirement, and he couldn't be happier.

"Well, I think you'll be fine. I just met my replacement, and he seems a lot nicer than me."

"Oh, I doubt that."

They chatted about their lives, about Ann's health, about Ben's last day—John even briefly mentioning how his son had shown up for Thanksgiving dinner. Both of them were drawing out the conversation as much as they could in order to delay their goodbye.

Finally Ben looked at his watch and sighed. "Well, I best be going. I wouldn't want to be too late on my last day."

John got up from his desk and shook Ben's hand as the two exchanged final goodbyes and then Ben headed down the hallway.

"Hey," John hollered as Ben turned the corner. "You know today's your last chance to jump that fence."

"You're right, I guess today has got to be the day," Ben responded with a large grin. And with that he gave a final wave and turned out of sight down the hallway.

John returned to his desk and shuffled some of his papers absentmindedly. It was a bit heartbreaking to see Ben go; he had become a real friend. John glanced outside the window and watched as Ben walked slowly alongside the fence.

Then, suddenly Ben stopped. He took his mailbag off of his shoulder and tossed it over the fence. He stared at the fence for a couple of seconds and then took about ten steps back. John couldn't believe his eyes, he almost threw open the window to warn Ben not to try it. Surely he was going to hurt himself. But before John could get to the window Ben bounded up to the fence and jumped straight over it. John nearly fell out of his chair as he watched Ben clear the fence easily, like he was an eighteen-year-old kid again hopping over a hurdle.

Ben jumped up and down on the other side like he was Rocky. He wore an expression of shock and excitement—he had clearly just surprised himself. After a few moments of celebration, Ben picked up his bag and began to head towards the next stop on his route. Before he was out of sight, Ben glanced back over his shoulder towards John's office window and flashed his biggest, brightest smile yet.

18

THE LAST STRAW

Growing up, Bobby was always a dreamer. Through his high school years, he kept a notebook and pen in his backpack so that he could write down whatever creative aspirations and audacious schemes came to his mind throughout the day. At night, he tucked the notebook and pen beneath his pillow so that when he awoke he could transcribe the many brilliant dreams that came to him as he slept.

But after Willie drowned, Bobby put the notebook and pen away. A poison had crept into his mind, turning his aspirations to doubts and his dreams to nightmares. He lost sight of the hopes he had for his future. They seemed distant and unattainable in the wake of disaster—a disaster that seemed to define his reality. At night, his fear of failing, his fear of being alone, and his fear of not being good enough would grip him as he lay awake tossing and turning. And when he finally did fall asleep, his fears would sweep in, manifesting themselves in his dreams.

During the day, whenever he stopped long enough to think about his life, he wouldn't dream of the future but spend every thought on past trauma. He thought about his family falling apart and how he had left them in their time of need. He thought about disappointing Aunt May and his father. He thought about God and how, if there even was a God, He must be so disappointed in Bobby. Even when Bobby was a kid, God was angry with him, and heck, he hadn't really done anything wrong yet. If God hated him back then, how angry must He be now? Bobby thought about how he had lost his morality, how he had become a drug dealer. And always, always, he would think about Willie.

So that's why Bobby had created himself a schedule that didn't allow the time for dreams: work, study, deal, party; repeat. For the past few years, it had become Bobby's entire lifestyle. Day after day, always the same thing: work, study, deal, party. He had learned how to drown out his thoughts by keeping active. He learned to keep from lying awake at night by running himself until he nearly collapsed from exhaustion. And he learned how to stop dreaming by never having more than a few hours to sleep. And for years it had worked rather effectively; that is, until the conversation with his father at Thanksgiving.

Bobby sipped beer from his red plastic cup as he sat to the side of his friend Tyler's crowded living room. "Living room" was a loose term considering it was more like an open, unfurnished trash heap in the middle of an all but demolished apartment. "Friend," an even looser term considering Tyler really was more of an acquaintance—an acquaintance that Bobby often spent time with, but hardly ever enjoyed.

Bobby had come to Tyler's party as more of an act of habit than actual social intent. Tyler, along with his kid brother Nelson, was a party animal with a perplexingly deep wallet and rabid drug habit. Their parties always involved a heavy amount of liquor, narcotics, and dangerous acts of idiotic entertainment. Considering that he always brought at least two of those three ingredients, Bobby was at the top of the brothers' invite list.

But on this particular day, Bobby had shown up empty-handed. Ever since his Thanksgiving dinner with his dad, Bobby had slowed his partying and drug dealing. And as he sat to the side of the room he found himself pondering upon his father's words. "I'm proud of you.... You're going to be quite a man someday." It had been over three months since Thanksgiving, and Bobby was still sorting out the meaning of those words.

The roar of the party encircled Bobby. Distorted music blared out of a blown-out speaker system. Partygoers screamed and shouted as they danced to the music. Tyler laughed with a few friends as they sat on a broken couch passing a joint back and forth. Nelson crashed through the house in a wasted tirade, picking up things and throwing them down.

Yet, despite all the noise, Bobby could only hear his own thoughts. *What did he see in me?* Bobby asked. In his mind, there was nothing he had ever done to deserve such words of confidence and admiration. If anyone else had said it, Bobby would have dismissed their words as meaningless, but he never knew his dad to say anything he didn't believe. The emotions that the words evoked in Bobby every time he thought back upon them were both acute and convoluted. It was inspiring for Bobby to think that his father had such hope in him. Yet it was also brutally heart-wrenching to not share those hopes in the least.

Bobby's thoughts were interrupted by a strong whiff of gasoline. He looked up to discover Nelson had taken an old gas canister from the garage and poured its contents all over himself in a drunken stupor. The rest of the partygoers seemed to either not care or not notice, but Bobby rose to his feet in concern. Nelson stumbled his way over to his brother.

"Light me!" He said with a thick slur in his speech.

Tyler looked at his brother with a grin and lit a match.

"Stop!" Bobby yelled from across the room—but it was too late. Nelson burst into flames. He screamed and slapped at himself trying to put out the flames as he ran for the front door. Tyler erupted into laughter as his brother tripped and fell on his way out the door. Bobby ran after the kid and helped him up and outside trying his best to not get burned, as well.

Once outside in the cold December night, Bobby threw Nelson into the snow that covered the yard.

"Roll around!" Bobby cried as Nelson screamed and writhed in pain. Bobby grabbed him and forced him to roll on the ground, finally smothering the flames in the snow.

Nelson gripped his face as he cried out in pain. Bobby turned to see Tyler meander out the door.

"What were you thinking?" Bobby screamed.

"Hey, he asked me to do it," Tyler said with a chuckle.

Bobby turned back to Nelson who still moaned in agony. His face was covered with red, blistering burns and his hands were a charred black. Bobby knelt down and picked him up and started to walk towards his car.

"Where are you going?" Tyler asked.

"To the hospital," Bobby responded without looking back.

"Oh come on, he'll be fine."

Bobby ignored Tyler's comments as he opened up his car and placed Nelson gently inside. By this time, most of the partygoers had walked outside and were silently watching. Bobby opened the driver's door but before he got in, he turned and looked over the crowd, many of whom were regular customers of Bobby's.

"I'm done," Bobby said loudly and forcefully. "If any of you come to me looking to buy, all you'll get from me is a black eye." Bobby looked directly at Tyler. "Do you hear me? I'm done with all of this." And with that, he sat down in his car, slammed the door, and sped off for the hospital.

19

HELL WEEK

A few weeks after the party, Bobby moved to Warrensburg, Missouri, to attend Central Missouri State University (CMSU). The last six months had been horrible, and the last six years had not been easy on him. But now it was a new season, a new chapter in his life, and a new opportunity to make something of himself. His decision to commit to a four-year school was as much a commitment against his old lifestyle as it was a resolution of a new one. He was moving on from his days of dealing drugs, stealing paintings, and cutting corners. He wasn't going to be afraid anymore; he wasn't going to fail anymore. He was going to finally make something of himself.

"You're going to be quite a man someday." The voice of his father had become a resounding source of strength for Bobby. The words were still hard for him to believe, but he was going to fight as hard as he could to make sure those words came true.

Bobby pushed open the doors to the mess hall and scanned the room looking for a familiar face. He found none. It was a bit weird for Bobby to be in an environment where everything and everyone was new to him. He got his lunch and re-scanned the tables looking for a group he could strike up a conversation with. A large round table full of short, ugly, and brawny brutes caught Bobby's attention. Broken noses, cauliflower ears, muscular frames without a shred of body fat—he knew a wrestler when he saw one, and here was a group of at least a dozen.

Bobby had joined the wrestling team but practices hadn't yet started, so Bobby figured he'd sit down and introduce himself to this band of soon-to-be brothers. As he sat down, he greeted the largest of the group, a young man who he would soon find out everyone called "Beast." Beast nodded and then after a few seconds, with a deep oaf-like voice, said, "Hey, watch this."

He popped out his left eye and dropped it into his glass of 7-Up. When Beast was a boy, he had lost his eye in a freak accident and had lived with a glass eyeball ever since. Apparently, he had become quite fond of popping his eye out from time to time to shock people.

Bobby watched the eye slowly sink down to the bottom, staring at him all along the way. He cracked a large grin. *I'm going to fit right in with these guys,* he thought.

—— – – ——

One hand locked onto the metal frame of the toilet paper dispenser inside of the fraternity's bathroom stall, the other hand gripping the wrist of the largest of the three men who had wrestled him down, Bobby held himself inches away from the toilet bowl as his captors attempted to give him a swirly. It was the fourth week of Bobby's first year at CMSU and the third day of "Hell Week," a four-day window of intense hazing within the fraternity that Bobby was attempting to join. Hell Week served as a sort of interview process that gave the fraternity brothers the opportunity to ruffle the feathers of the new recruits to see what they were made of. So far, all the group had deduced about Bobby was that he was incredibly hard to haze.

He flailed his legs in the air as the three seniors did their best to force his head into the toilet. Over the past few days, they had already tried unsuccessfully to give Bobby a swirly three times and were finding it to be a rather difficult undertaking. Bobby's flailing knee connected with one of the frat boy's noses. He winced in pain but kept a firm grip on Bobby—they couldn't let him get away again.

"For the love of God, do not let him go!" one of the seniors yelled to the others.

Bobby took both of his hands and gripped the rim of the toilet bowl. Sure, hazing was a part of joining any fraternity and it's not like he could avoid it forever—he knew this. He held himself up as the three seniors pushed down with all their strength. It just would have been too easy to play along; he had to put up at least some sort of fight. He suddenly tucked his head underneath the toilet and flipped his legs forward, crashing his back into the toilet but also throwing two of the seniors smack against the back wall. Bobby grabbed hold of the third senior and wrestled him to the ground.

It was a pretty straight-forward formula: the more he fought, the more he irritated the fraternity brothers; the more irritated they were, the worse the hazing would be. But it was just not in Bobby's nature to let someone bully him. If they were going to haze him, they would have to try harder than this. Bobby rolled out of the stall and headed out the bathroom door.

That afternoon, Bobby took a couple of textbooks and a lamp, and slid under his dorm room bed. The fraternity made it a very specific point to not allow any hazing after Hell Week had ended so as to keep initiation from getting too out of hand. Bobby checked his watch as he situated himself underneath the bed: only eight more hours before Hell Week was over—their window was closing fast. It was just a matter of time before they came busting into his dorm to drag him out God knows where to do God knows what. But until they did, he might as well be productive. He clicked on the lamp and began to pore over his textbooks while listening intently for the slightest stir.

Every once in a while he would hear something—someone walking by in the hallway, a knock on a door a couple of rooms down—and would immediately switch the lamp off and keep as quiet as possible until he was sure it was safe to click the light on again. For hours it went like this until finally,

BAM!

The sound of Bobby's door swinging open and hitting the wall caused him to jerk up and hit his head on the metal bed frame. Ignoring the pain he reached over and flicked off the lamp with one quick fluid movement. He held his breath and listened as several sets of feet came running into his room.

"Ah come on! He's not here!" Bobby recognized the voice as one of the seniors who had tried to give him a swirly earlier that day.

He heard several groans. By Bobby's count there were at least four guys in the room.

"Well where do you think he is?"

"I don't know, maybe studying at the library. You two go and check, and we will stay here in case he comes back."

The old rusty springs creaked as the senior sat down on Bobby's small bed. For a moment Bobby thought of how funny it would be if he suddenly popped out from under the bed and grabbed the senior's leg. Bobby checked his watch and suppressed his temptation; he just had a few more hours to go.

"Do we even want this guy in our fraternity?" one of the frat brothers questioned.

"Well apparently he is pretty good wrestler," the senior responded.

"We've got plenty of good wrestlers...we don't need him."

"Plenty of wrestlers with good grades? I mean I'm not sure if I really like the guy either but he is dedicated, I'll give him that. Every time I go to the library he is in there studying his butt off."

The senior's words caught Bobby off guard. Bobby hadn't thought about it a whole lot, but it was true, he had been spending a lot of time at the library. While growing up, school had never been that big of a priority for him. Through middle school and high school he was all about getting through with as little effort as possible. But now, even though it was still pretty early in the year, it was clear something had changed. He was not only passing, he was excelling. It wasn't new for him to be fighting for something; there was never a question that Bob Hartley was always going to fight, it was just a question of what he was fighting for. And the fact that he was now fighting for something so substantial—it lifted his spirit to think about it. When he first applied to CMSU, it was for the sole intention of getting out of town and lying low. But now his motivation had changed; he was actually giving his all to his education: fighting to learn, fighting to grow, and fighting to change.

"So, I guess we are going to let him in?" The continuing conversation between the fraternity brothers brought Bobby back to the moment.

"We have the lowest average GPA out of any fraternity at this school. We could use an egghead like this guy."

Egghead. Well there is a name I've never been called before.

The bed creaked again as the senior got up.

"Okay, I have things I have to do," he said with a sigh. "I say we just come back and check for him again in a couple hours."

The dorm room door groaned as they pushed it open and walked out into the hallway. Bobby cracked a triumphant smirk and began to breathe easier as the footsteps faded down the hallway.

"Hey fellas," Someone greeted the frat brothers as they passed in the hallway. "What are you doing here?" The voice belonged to Bobby's roommate, a tall, goofy-looking freshman whom Bobby had remarked, on several occasions, looked like he belonged to the Adams Family.

"Ah, we were just looking for your roommate," the senior responded.

"Oh yeah, he's been trying to hide from you guys. He's probably underneath his bed."

—— - - ——

Bobby took a breath of the fresh air as he glanced in every direction. White snow covered the cornfields that stretched for miles toward the east and blanketed the rolling hills to the south. The sun painted an elegant red glow as it dipped below the western horizon. Not a single road, house, or person was in sight. Normally, Bobby would have appreciated such a beautiful and serene picture. But, considering he was handcuffed to a large metal bed frame with absolutely no idea where he was, well, he just wasn't really in the mood.

When the fraternity brothers had figured out that he was hiding underneath his bed, they ran into his dorm room and attempted to drag him out. But Bobby immediately latched onto his bed frame and no matter how hard they tried to pry him loose, he didn't let go. So they grabbed a pair of handcuffs, cuffed him to the bed frame, dragged both him and the bedframe out of the dorm room and into the back of a pickup truck, drove several miles out of town, and then dumped him in the middle of an empty field and left him there.

The bed frame rattled as Bobby dragged it across the field. He looked to the ground where two flattened strips of snow outlined the path in which the fraternity brothers had driven off. *How far out did they leave me?* He asked himself as he did his best to recall how long it had taken them to get out there. *It was a long drive... at least twenty minutes.* They had blindfolded him just before they threw him in the back of the truck so that he could only guess the path they had taken. Perhaps they had taken longer, just looping around on random roads to throw him off. Regardless though, it was going to be a long walk back and the sun had already hidden itself underneath the horizon. He was going to have to move quickly, which was turning out to be pretty difficult to do while handcuffed to a metal bed frame.

After only about five minutes of walking, Bobby stopped and set down the bed. *Yeah, I am not going to make it back.* It wasn't like him to give up so quickly, but then again, it was pretty clear that he was going nowhere fast, and stumbling around in the dark handcuffed to a bed seemed like it could be a bit dangerous. Stars had begun to glimmer as the sky dimmed. He sat down on top of the bed frame and sighed. When life gives you lemons you make lemonade, and when life dumps you in the middle of a field handcuffed to a bed frame in the middle of January, you sleep out under the stars hoping you don't die of hypothermia.

"Hey, Bulldog," said a voice, cutting the silence and causing Bobby to nearly jump out of skin. He whipped around to see Beast standing just a few paces off.

"Whoa! Hey, where did you come from?" Bobby responded, startled.

"I followed the truck. I figured you would need some help," Beast explained with his booming monotone voice.

"Wait, so you can take me back?"

Beast nodded and then pointed behind him.

"My car's behind that hill. I'll help you carry the bed over."

Bobby stood up and headed immediately toward the hill. "Oh don't worry about it, Beast. I got it."

As the two walked over the hill Bobby saw Beast's car sitting on the side of a gravel road and immediately his elation stalled.

Beast stated the obvious. "I have a very small car."

"Yeah, I see that."

Bobby glanced at his gigantic friend. "How do you even fit in there?"

"I duck."

Bobby nodded. "Okay, well, we can make this work."

Bobby slipped his body through the passenger window and into the car, then, using his handcuffed arm, held the bed upside down on top of the roof. As they drove down the gravel road, an occasional bump would send the bed sliding down the back of the car nearly ripping Bobby's arm off. But they would just stop, reset, and then start again. It was a long process, but it beat walking back.

Eventually, they made it back to the main road and the ride got smoother. As they pulled up next to a stoplight, Bobby made eye contact with the driver of an adjacent car. A perplexed and moderately amused look crossed the driver's face as he stared at the bed frame sitting unattached atop the car's roof.

"How are you doing?" Bobby courteously asked with a nod.

—— – – ——

"Classic, man, classic," one of the fraternity brothers said to another, slapping him on the back as they headed back into their frat house. After finally and successfully hazing Bobby, they had stopped to get celebratory drinks on the way back.

"Did you see his face as we drove off?" the senior said, as he pushed open the door. "Oh man, it's going to take him forever to—" His voice trailed off.

The rest of the fraternity brothers stopped dead in their tracks. Sitting quietly on their couch, Bobby, still handcuffed to the bed frame, pretended not to notice them as he thumbed through the pages of a book he held in his hands.

"Oh," Bobby exclaimed, finally looking up. "Hey fellas."

20

SPINNING OUT OF CONTROL

Clack! Clack! Clack!

The persistent sound of tapping came from Bobby's second-floor window, jolting him from a deep slumber. Bobby rolled over groggily to check the time: three in the morning.

Clack! Clack! Clack!

This time it was louder. For the first time in months, Bobby had actually gotten to bed at a decent hour and had the opportunity to get a full night of sleep. It was the summer break after his freshman year at CMSU and, true to Bob Hartley form, he was working three jobs over the summer so he could have money for the next school year.

Cherishing his much-needed sleep, he had even unplugged his phone just before going to bed so he could avoid any interruptions. Bobby cursed whoever it was knocking against his window and remained motionless, hoping it would go away.

Clack! Clack! Clack!

In a rush of anger, Bobby tossed off his covers and ran to his window to investigate. He arrived just in time to see a rock the size of a golf ball fly up and hit his window. He looked down to see someone standing in the yard tossing rocks.

"What are you doing?" Bobby asked as he stuck his head out the window, dodging another flying rock.

"Where is my package?" the man screamed. It was dark, and Bobby couldn't see the face of the screaming man, but he recognized his voice immediately. One of his three jobs was a nightly route delivering packages. And the man who now stood fuming beneath Bobby's window was Danny, the owner and manager of the delivery company. Danny was always angry, always dissatisfied, and always on edge. Although small in stature, he held himself with a terrifying and imposing presence. Napoleonic in both appearance and attitude, Danny stood just above five feet tall and had a hairline that receded so far back, he had to press his chin to his neck and strain his eyes upward to catch any glimpse of it in the mirror.

Bobby looked down at Danny—his round bald head had flushed red with anger. "Danny, I don't know what you are talking about. What package?" Bobby responded.

"The small box I gave you!"

Suddenly, Bobby remembered. Earlier that day, when he was loading up his truck to go on a delivery route, Danny had approached him and given him an extra package to deliver. Bobby had taken the package, tossed it in his truck's cab, and had completely forgotten about it until now.

Bobby ran downstairs, not bothering to put on shoes or a coat. He ran out to his car and rifled through his truck cab, finally finding the package tucked beneath the passenger seat.

"You have to get that delivered right now!" Danny said, as looked over Bobby's shoulder.

"I'm sorry. Look, I'll take it first thing tomorrow." Bobby said, exhausted and having no desire to actually go back to work.

"Did you read the address? You have to take that to Saint Luke's Hospital! Inside that package is a pacemaker; some doctor called me saying they were waiting for it so they could go into surgery!"

Finally understanding the magnitude of his mistake, Bobby jumped back into his car, not wasting another moment.

"Well, now he's in a hurry," Danny said, as he tossed his hands in the air. "I wouldn't worry about it; the patient is probably dead already!" He yelled sarcastically as Bobby peeled out and headed to the hospital.

Bobby arrived minutes later to find several doctors waiting for him. He handed them the package and after giving him a couple disapproving looks, they ran back inside to perform the surgery.

Bobby never found out for sure, but he assumed the surgery was successful. At the very least, he was never called in by the city for another wrongful death suit.

When he returned home, he found a note plastered on his door.

"Call me when you read this. I need you to fill in later today. You owe me—Danny."

Bobby sighed. That evening he was actually free and had been really looking forward to having a night off so he could get some rest. He had packed his schedule so tightly that very rarely did he get a full night's sleep.

Bobby picked his phone up, plugged it back into the wall, and reluctantly gave Danny a call.

"Hey, Danny, this is Bobby—"

"We have some extra packages and I need you to deliver them this afternoon—"

Bobby interrupted Danny mid-sentence.

"I can't, I work from eight to five at one of my other jobs."

"Then you'll come in at quarter after five." Danny wasn't going to take no for an answer.

"I haven't gotten any sleep." Bobby tried to explain.

"You screwed up today, Bobby. You owe me." Without waiting for an answer, Danny hung up.

Bobby glanced at the clock—five in the morning. He could still get a couple of hours of sleep in. Bobby checked his sock drawer to make sure he still had some truckers. He was going to need them.

Three hours into his delivery route it had started to get dark outside, and Bobby struggled to keep himself awake. He was stretching himself beyond the boundaries of mere exhaustion and was stepping into near delirium.

It had become actually fairly common for Bobby to doze off while driving. He had been in a couple of near accidents due to falling asleep while driving, but had always managed to snap awake just in time to hit the brakes, or to veer away from oncoming traffic. However, this night, Bobby was so tired, he knew if he dozed off it would be hard for him to wake up immediately.

Every few minutes that passed added weight to Bobby's eyes even though he fought desperately to keep them open. His vision danced in and out of a hazy blur. With only about an hour left on his route, Bobby was winding his way down an empty back road when his mind began playing tricks on him. His eyes blurred and the light emanating from the street lights suddenly looked as if it was coming from the headlights of oncoming traffic. Startled, he jerked the wheel, trying to avoid a head-on collision.

His truck spun out of control and slammed into the curb, flipping onto its roof and skidding across the street. Turned upside down, everything inside the truck was tossed around the cab. Bobby ducked instinctively as a tire jack he kept behind his back seat flew up against the roof and landed just inches away from his head.

After sliding for several meters upside down, the truck finally came to a stop, tires spinning wildly in the air. For a few seconds, Bobby didn't move as he hung upside down in the car. He just remained motionless staring at the car jack that had come so incredibly close to bashing him in the head. A quiet electronic ding came from dash, alerting Bobby to the fact that one of the doors was ajar. Bobby wiped his face as blood trickled from his chin down across forehead.

Can cars catch on fire after flipping? The thought hit Bobby like the buzz of a morning alarm waking him from a deep slumber. Finally finding himself back in the moment, he jerked up, unbuckled his seatbelt and tried to open the door, but it was jammed. Full of adrenaline, Bobby smashed his front windshield and pulled himself up and out of wreckage.

After running what he considered a safe distance away, Bobby stopped and sat down on the curb to catch his breath. As the adrenaline rush began to fade, Bobby looked himself over to see if he was alright. Amazingly, besides a small cut on his chin and one on each of his hands from crawling out of the wreckage, he seemed to be just fine. But Bobby wasn't fine, not in the least bit. He had lived through the event unscathed but the intensity of the moment had reopened a wound in his soul. Suddenly, his emotions boiled over.

Bobby dropped his head into his hands, completely defeated and distraught. He tried to calm his breathing and slow his racing heart, but it took all of his effort just to keep from completely breaking down. Tears rolled down his face as he became more aware of how narrowly he had just escaped death. He kept his face buried in hands; there was no one around, but still he didn't want anyone seeing him in such a devastated and emotional state.

For years, Bobby's life had been spinning out of his control, and now he had just nearly killed himself by doing just that: spinning out of control.

"Why can't you get a grip?" Bobby screamed at himself, suddenly not caring if anyone saw or heard him.

The only reason he was still alive was just simple, stupid, dumb luck. He easily could be lying dead in that truck. He had spent the last year of his life getting his act together. He had cleaned himself up, started to make good grades, and stopped drug dealing. And yet here he was, still without an ounce of control of his life. Thoughts of self-hatred crept into his mind. He thought about how no one would have really cared had he died; he thought about how no one really should've cared if he had died. He thought about his inability to ever control his life. *No matter how hard I try, I am always going to fail.*

He tightened his fist and punched the cement beneath him.

"Get a hold of yourself!" he screamed aloud.

His emotions brought him back to the moment when Little Willie's head dropped and the boy went limp in his arms. The memory of such helplessness and defeat stuck inside of him like an incurable disease.

But then out of nowhere, a voice that was not his own rang out clearly in his head.

"I died for you happily." A chill ran down Bobby's spine as the voice boomed with a beautiful and haunting fortitude. A calming presence settled over him. He had felt this presence before, years earlier in the cubbyhole at church, except now he was too old to play pretend. But, was it pretend? The voice was as clear as anything Bobby had ever heard in his life, as if it came from someone sitting right next to him.

The words hit Bobby as hard as his truck had hit the curb. He buried his face into his hands, weeping now for a different reason. His thoughts of anger, self-hatred, and pain faded into the background as this voice, which was all too real, spoke out again.

"I died for you happily," the voice repeated.

Bobby had no words to describe what it was that he felt at the moment the voice spoke to him. He had no idea where it was coming from—maybe it was just his own mind playing tricks on him or maybe stress and sleep-deprivation were causing a delusion. He didn't have any idea, but all he knew was that he no longer felt alone as he sat on the side of the road. And as tangibly as he heard the voice in his head, Bobby suddenly felt the physical presence of someone sitting next to him. A comforting arm wrapped around Bobby's shoulder as he kept his eyes shut and his face buried. He did not look up, because he was afraid that what he would see would be beyond what he could understand.

Then the voice changed, not in tone, but in message. The voice repeated the words of Bobby's father at Thanksgiving.

"I'm proud of you Bobby. You're going to be quite a man someday, and you will touch a lot of lives."

The words possessed a new authority as they deposited a new truth in Bobby's heart. He nodded and dared to believe it was actually true. *One day I'm going to be quite a man,* Bobby thought. *One day....*

And then, as suddenly as it had arrived, the presence and the voice left, and Bobby looked up to find himself alone. He sat there confused and overwhelmed. He wondered if he had just dreamed it all; maybe while he had his head buried in his arms, he had fallen asleep for just a split second. *It had to have been a dream,* he thought. But whatever it was, it had left Bobby with a profound sense of comfort.

——— – – ———

It took nearly thirty minutes before Bobby called Danny to fill him in on what had happened. He had to walk a couple of blocks before finding a working pay phone.

"Alright, I'll be there in ten minutes," Danny said, after exchanging some coarse words.

Bobby started to jog back to the crash. He wanted this night to be over; he wanted to go home. Whatever had just happened exceeded his comprehension, and he had no ability to process it.

Rounding the corner, Bobby looked at his truck which still lay belly up in the middle of the road. Two thoughts then crossed Bobby's mind in immediate succession. *Nope, still didn't blow up*—provoking just a touch of disappointment. The second—*It's in the middle of the road...should I have called the police?*

Danny showed up shortly in his own delivery truck and hopped out.

"What in God's name were you doing Bobby?" Danny said as he surveyed the damage in disbelief.

"Do you think we should call the police?" Bobby asked.

"I'll take care of all of that; you take care of the packages," Danny responded, leaving Bobby a bit confused.

"What packages?"

"The ones you have in the back there!" Danny said while shoving a short round finger towards the truck.

"You want me to take them back to the dock?"

Danny began to lose his temper "No, you idiot, I want you to finish your delivery! What, do you just think you get to clock out now? We guarantee overnight delivery."

"You can't be serious."

Danny threw open the back of Bobby's truck as he now had completely lost his temper. He rattled of a constant spout of livid degradation toward Bobby, calling him a list of names that would make a sailor shudder. However, only one word actually affected Bobby: "worthless."

Bobby walked over to the back of his truck and pulled out a roll of packing tape as Danny continued his endless tirade. Bobby reached over and locked both of Danny's arms with one of his own, using the other to take the tape and wrap it multiple times around Danny's mouth.

"You talk too much." Bobby said, as he spun the tape around Danny's mouth for the third time. Danny's eyes had all but popped out of his round head and Bobby could see the anger contained therein.

Bobby dropped the tape, let go of Danny, and began to walk home. "And I'm not worthless," he said, not looking back.

21

"GOD IS GOOD!"

Three years after first arriving at CMSU, and now midway through his senior year in college, Bobby had completely turned his life around. His days of drug dealing, stealing, and underachieving were far behind him. He was just a single point below a perfect GPA, two time winner of CMSU's outstanding athlete award, and a member of the student relations council. He had set out to change his life, and change it he had.

Instead of the many destructive relationships he had built in the past, Bobby had begun making friends whom he believed he could really count on. He wanted to be someone whom he could be proud of, to be someone who achieved great things—and to do that, he knew he needed to surround himself with like-minded individuals.

One such individual was a man named Steve Collins. Steve was also a member of CMSU's student relations council and after collectively launching several initiatives together, Bobby and Steve had become fast friends. Within a few weeks of meeting him, Steve had immediately struck Bobby as one of the wisest individuals he had ever met. He seemed to have a solution to every problem that would arise during the meetings, and he was never at a loss for a profound word.

"How do you come up with all of these answers?" Bobby had once asked Steve during one of their meetings.

"They are all in here," Steve said, pulling a Bible out of his bag and raising it up.

"Well, I guess no one is perfect," Bobby responded in a light, teasing manner.

But even though he was joking, there was a measure of disdain in Bobby's knee-jerk reaction. For him, faith was full of painful memories of disappointment and failures. Religion was a closed chapter in his book that he had no desire to reopen.

But despite their differences, Bobby and Steve grew to be close friends. So when Steve showed up at Bobby's door with dinner in hand one night toward the end of the first semester of his senior year, Bobby didn't even think twice before inviting Steve in.

"It would be a fantastic experience, and you would learn a whole lot!" Steve said with the same charismatic enthusiasm he seemed to always carry. They had both just about finished their dinner, and Steve was now trying to convince Bobby to attend a leadership conference held in Chicago the following week. But despite Steve's conviction, Bobby's thoughts drifted.

Glancing about his dining room, Bobby noticed how different the decor in his house had become over the past five years. He no longer had a single stolen panting, black light poster, or knife throwing decorating his walls. There simply wasn't room. His walls were too full with various plaques and trophies he had collected over the course of time at CMSU.

There was a medal he had been awarded after being labeled CMSU's most outstanding athlete, a framed article from the college's newspaper giving rave reviews to the collegiate TV show Bobby hosted, countless wrestling awards, and a trophy for winning the school's handball tournament. He even had a plaque commemorating his victory at the school's annual beer-chugging competition—twenty-two beers in less than thirty minutes had made a school record.

"Come on, I think you'd really enjoy it," Steve said as the two finished up their dinner. "Plus it ends on Friday, so you'll have the whole weekend to enjoy downtown Chicago!"

Bobby listened half-heartedly as he carried their dishes to the kitchen.

"I'm just not sure why you want me to go so bad," Bobby said as he opened his kitchen window.

"Because I think it could be really good for you, and—"

Steve stopped mid-sentence as he watched Bobby toss the whole stack of dishes out of the back window. They landed with a deafening metallic crash.

"I don't have a dishwasher," Bobby said with a casual shrug. "That's why I bought metal dishes. I have a power washer in the back so I can just use that to clean them."

Steve shook his head and laughed. He had known Bobby for months and was still astounded by him daily. Steve continued.

"You by no means have to go. I just think it will be a good learning experience and I already have two passes so it wouldn't cost you at all."

Bobby shrugged.

"Alright, I'll think about it."

—— – – ——

Two steps inside of the conference, and Bobby was already sure he had made the right decision in attending. Apparently the conference had been marketed extremely well to twenty-something women, because never before had Bobby seen a place so full of attractive young ladies. Bernie, a fellow CMSU wrestler who had also been convinced by Steve to attend the conference, gave Bobby a nudge as they walked to their seats.

"Well, would you look at that," Bernie said with an ear-to-ear grin. "Looks like this might not be that bad after all."

Originally, Steve had planned on going with Bobby to the conference, but something had come up and he had bowed out last minute, convincing Bernie to come in his place. Bobby had nearly backed out of the trip altogether after finding out Bernie was coming instead. Even though he was a fellow wrestler, Bernie just struck Bobby as being a total meathead. It seemed as if Bernie had never had a deep or original thought in his life. Talking with him felt about as intellectually and philosophically stimulating as talking to a cheeseburger. If you weren't talking about girls, food, or wrestling—Bernie just wasn't interested.

Bobby didn't want to encourage Bernie so he did his best to ignore his comment. But he couldn't help but cracking a little smile. This was shaping up better than he had expected.

The lights in the auditorium dimmed just as the two found their seats. A spotlight beamed down upon the stage, and a man with pearly white teeth and a dimpled smile walked up to the podium.

"God is good!" He shouted in to the microphone.

What? What is this guy talking about? Bobby looked around confused.

In unison, the crowd around Bobby responded, "All the time!"

"And all the time?" the man at the podium said, still not breaking his smile.

"God is good!" the crowd echoed.

No, no, no, please tell me this isn't what I think it is. Bobby met eyes with Bernie who shared the same worried look.

The man at the podium continued. "Well alright. My name is Pastor David and I would like to thank you all for attending our Campus Crusade for Christ Leadership Conference!"

Campus Crusade for Christ? Never had Steve once mentioned this being a Christian conference. Bobby thought back on Steve's many invitations. *"Bobby come to this Leadership Conference, it'll be good for you."* Bobby shook his head in disbelief. *No wonder he wanted me to go so bad.*

Bobby scanned the auditorium. Hundreds of young adults with smiles plastered on their faces were scribbling in their leather bound journals with such ferocity you would think they were in some sort of competition.

Bobby glanced over to see Bernie had already checked out, his head resting on the back of the chair, mouth gaping open, and eyes sealed shut. For a few moments, Bobby thought he would do the same. But no, he had come to this conference for a reason. He reached down into his bag and pulled out his notebook and pen. *Even if I disagree with every single thing he says, I'm still learning something from this conference. I didn't come all the way up to Chicago for nothing.*

Pastor David mentioned a passage and, immediately, the shuffle of hundreds of Bibles opening and pages turning filled the room.

It was hard for Bobby to keep up with the speaker; he would mention a passage but not read it, or he would mention a name or a story from the Bible but wouldn't explain it. It was similar to when Bobby had accidentally showed up to an advanced Spanish class instead of the introductory course—they were not speaking his language, and Bobby was as lost as could be.

It was clear that this was not a conference intended for the general public. This was a full-blown, grew-up-in-a-Christian-household, went-to-Sunday-school, attended-Bible-college kind of conference. There was a lot of jargon that was foreign to him, but as Pastor David continued to share, Bobby started to get the big picture of what he was saying. Essentially, the message was about evangelism and sharing the gospel. Pastor David would give key phrases and then the crowd would nod their heads. Bobby would then write down the phrase doing his best to decipher what it meant.

"We are the body of Christ, and you and I are to be his hands and feet." = *Our job in life is to do what Jesus told us to do.*

"We are called to be in the world but not of it." = *You can be around nonbelievers and preach to them, but make sure you stay away from sex, drugs, and rock and roll.*

"He is the way, the truth, and the life, and no one gets to the Father except through him." = *Believe in Jesus or you are going to go to hell.*

Some of these phrases he had heard before, and some of them were new. The more he listened, the more it seemed as if it was just the same basic Christian stuff, only some of it was repackaged to sound more poetic. But then Pastor David said something that Bobby hadn't heard before, at least not from a pulpit.

"God is a good God who loves us. He believes in us, and He sent his Spirit to lead us and guide us." He said it so matter-of-factly and with such confidence, as if he was telling the crowd that the sun would rise the next morning.

Now this was too much for Bobby; he immediately stood up and exclaimed, "No, that's not true!"

It was only after this first sentence that Bobby realized what he was doing—but by then it was too late to turn back. The speaker had stopped and the whole crowd had turned and looked at him.

"You say He loves us," Bobby shook his head and then continued, equaling if not surpassing Pastor David's level of confidence and conviction, "It's not true. He doesn't care about us at all."

And with that, he sat back down.

—— - - ——

After bumbling through the rest of his notes, obviously thrown by Bobby's interruption, Pastor David closed the session in a prayer and released everyone for lunch. Just as he was getting up from his seat, a young woman approached Bobby, skipping introductions and diving straight into discussion. "I think you have a wrong picture of who Christ is," she told him in a tone that was one part compassion and two parts correction. "He *is* good. And you have no idea how much He loves you!"

She pulled out a Bible and thumbed through it quickly. The pages were all lit up by layers of penned-in notes and highlighted passages.

"You know it kind of defeats the purpose if you highlight everything," Bobby said with a chuckle as he looked at her colorful pages.

Ignoring Bobby's comment, she continued. "See in Ephesians 2 it says, '*But God, being rich in mercy, because of the great love with which he loved us, even when we were dead in our trespasses, made us alive with Christ—*'" but before she could finish, Bobby interrupted her.

"Look, if there is a God, He doesn't want to have anything to do with us. And He certainly doesn't love us, least of all me."

"But He really does," she insisted.

"No," Bobby said with an absolute firmness. "No. I can tell you, without a doubt, He most certainly does not."

He then turned and walked off. Immediately afterwards, another individual approached him and struck up a nearly identical conversation. In fact, during the course of the conference, Bobby must have had dozens of such discussions. It made sense: he was a non-believer attending a Christian leadership conference centered on evangelism, and moreover, he had stood up in the middle of the conference and openly rejected one of their core beliefs. Of course everyone wanted to meet him, talk to him, and see if they could change his mind.

Each time someone would start the conversation with him, they led with an assertion of the good and loving nature of God. Maybe they would use a Bible verse, perhaps a story from Scripture, or even a testament of how God had been good to them in their own life. But it didn't matter to Bobby; it was all empty rhetoric. No matter what they said, it didn't change what he had seen in his own life. Everything Bobby had ever deduced about the nature of God was that He was a God who was nowhere to be found.

22

THE CHICAGO HOTEL ROOM

"Look, there are only a couple more sessions. You have to make it to at least one more," Bobby said to Bernie the morning of the third and final day of the conference.

To save on costs, the two were sharing a hotel room together, and Bobby had nearly reached his limit with Bernie. Once Bernie had realized that not a single girl at the conference wanted to talk about anything other than Jesus, he had stopped attending altogether. Instead, he spent his entire time goofing off around the hotel or hopping from bar to bar.

"Whatever, man, I know you have the whole weekend here but my flight leaves this afternoon and I am not spending my last day in downtown Chicago going to some Bible-thumping conference," Bernie said, as he walked into the bathroom to brush his teeth.

"Then I don't even understand why you came out here. You know, Steve had to pay to get us into this conference right?" Bobby said, as he got up and stood in the doorway of the bathroom.

"Yeah, well he didn't ever inform me what the conference was actually going to be about," Bernie paused as he stuck his toothbrush in his mouth. "Besides, it's not like I would be learning anything if I went," he said with his mouth full of toothpaste.

"That's not true. Even if you disagree with everything they are saying, there is still something you could be learning," Bobby asserted.

Bernie spit and then rinsed. "Yeah and what is it that you've been learning?"

Bobby paused. In all reality, he hadn't learned much of anything during the conference. He had countless discussions about the nature of God, but each one had been more like a Ping-Pong match than a discussion. Someone would make a statement about the nearness of the Holy Spirit to Bobby and then he would tell them that, although it was a nice thought, it just wasn't true. The conversation would then go on, sometimes even for hours, but really, they would never evolve beyond that disagreement.

"Face it, man, God is just a made-up idea," Bernie said as he walked over to the toilet and lifted the lid and began to relieve himself. Bobby turned to face the other direction. "God is nothing more than just a sad, sick trick mankind has pulled on itself. And anyone one who is delusional enough to believe it doesn't have anything to offer me," Bernie finished.

Something about this statement nearly drove Bobby past his breaking point. Although he completely disagreed with the idea of a good-natured and present God, the existence of God was something he had at least pondered. He could not definitively say, beyond a shadow of a doubt, that God was real. However something inside of him always seemed to ache a resounding confirmation toward His existence.

"Bernie, you really shouldn't be so selective about the people you want to learn from, because let's face it, you are a moron. There are monkeys who probably know more about life then you do...." Bobby's words trailed off as he realized Bernie had turned away from the toilet and now was peeing directly on Bobby's shoes.

Moments later, a bellman from the adjacent hotel happened to glance up across the street in time to see Bobby dump Bernie's suitcase full of clothes outside the window of their eighteenth story hotel room.

——— – – ———

That evening, after the conference had ended, Bobby returned to his hotel to eat dinner. He hadn't completely formulated his plan for the weekend, but he was looking forward to the opportunity to go out and see the city. As he sat down at the hotel's bar and grill, he noticed an elderly gentleman eating alone in a side booth while poring over a Bible he had out on top of his table. Bobby figured the man must've also been in town to attend the leadership conference. The hotel and the conference center were just a block away from each other and Bobby had already seen several individuals at both places. So when his food came, Bobby picked up his plate and walked over to older gentleman's booth.

"Do you mind if I join you?"

At first the gentleman was caught off guard by Bobby's sudden approach, but he smiled a gentle smile and nodded.

"I saw you reading your Bible, and I just wondered if I could ask you a couple of questions," Bobby asked, immediately following up his question with, "My name's Bobby, by the way." He extended his hand.

"George," the man responded, with a thick English accent. "And yes, you can ask me any questions you want."

For the next several hours, Bobby talked with George about everything he had been pondering about the nature of God over the past week. All in all, it was less of a dialog and more of Bobby verbally processing things he never found resolution to—but George didn't seem to mind one bit. He never looked at his watch and never made Bobby feel pressured for time; he just listened patiently to every word that spilled out of Bobby's heart.

And then, in contrast to the knee-jerk answers at the conference, George thought carefully before answering. He gave simple yet profound answers that surprised Bobby. After several hours, Bobby finally found himself rounding back to the primary question he tossed around ever since coming to the conference.

"It's just, if God is good," he said as he shook his head, "I mean if He really is like they say He is, well then, why was He never there for me?" Now, for the first time, Bobby was actually asking the question with a desire to find the answer.

George thought. Bobby had asked a genuine question and he was searching for a genuine answer.

"Bobby," he finally said, "I...don't know." George then smiled as he continued. "It is a great question to ask. It really is. I'm just not the one you should be asking," George said as he set his hand on his Bible. "Maybe you need to ask Him where He was."

Bobby nodded as he digested George's answer. "I'm not sure how." Bobby couldn't remember ever praying before.

"Sure you do. It is no different than asking these questions to me," George replied. "Just talk to Him."

Bobby smiled and stood up to leave. "Yeah, maybe I will." He reached out and shook George's hand. "It really was nice to meet you, George."

"My pleasure."

"Now that the conference is over, are you headed home?" Bobby said, feeling the need to close with some cordial conversation.

"Well, I am headed home tomorrow, but I didn't come here for any conference. I came to Chicago to visit family," George informed him.

"You weren't here for the leadership conference?" Bobby looked at him, shocked. "So you had no idea who I was or what I was talking about when I first sat down?"

"I must admit, I was a tad confused," George said with a chuckle.

Bobby shook his head. "Huh. Wow. So it was just a coincidence or something that you were here at the same time as me?"

George nodded and smiled. "Must've been."

——— – – ———

That night, Bobby knelt beside the bed in his Chicago hotel room, hands clasped and eyes shut, doing his best to posture himself in what he figured was the correct prayer stance. For several minutes, he didn't say anything—he didn't know what to say. How was he supposed to start? He had learned the Lord's Prayer years ago when he was kid. He wondered if he should perhaps start with that, but then gave up on the idea when he realized he probably only could recite about a third of it.

He then thought back to the advice George gave him. *"Just talk with Him."* Bobby shrugged. "Alright, why not," he said aloud. He felt uncomfortable speaking aloud with no one else in the room.

He thought for a moment about the room's next door. *Can anyone hear me? They are going to think I'm nuts if they can hear me.* But Bobby pushed the thought of his head and continued on.

"God, if you are real, and if you really are the God they say you are, well, I'm not leaving this room until I meet You for myself." Bobby felt like he was out looking for buried treasure. He knew it probably was going to turn out to be nothing. He knew this searching was probably going to end up being nothing more than a waste of time. *But then again, what if it isn't? What if there really is gold at the end of this journey?* His rational mind and past experiences told him otherwise, but he still just desperately needed to find out the truth. If there really was a good and loving God out there, he had to discover that God for himself.

"They say you are a good God, but I don't know. If You are good, then why have You never helped me?" Bobby asked, his voice bouncing off the walls of the tiny room. It was odd to hear questions that had echoed in his head for so long finally be given an actual voice.

"If You really do love me, then why have You not shown it?" After each question, Bobby paused and waited for an answer, even though he didn't expect to ever get one.

"If You cared about me, then why were You never there for me?" Tears began to well up in his eyes. He had spent all of his life bottling up his memories, and over the past few days, it was as if someone had taken that bottle and shaken it up—so as he took the lid off, everything began exploding out.

"Where were You when my mother was in pain?" Pictures flooded his mind of how his mother would scream out in agony every time she moved. Suddenly, Bobby was up off of his knees and on his feet pacing back and forth across the small room with a focused determination.

"She never did anything to deserve something like that, and yet it happened to her anyway. Where were You during any of that?" Bobby again waited for an answer but only heard silence.

"Where were You when her pain caused her to lash out in anger? When she took out her anger on my family, on me?" His voice grew louder as the pain of the memories grew stronger. "When my family began to fall apart, and I had to move out, where were You? I was just a kid and had to make it in the world all on my own—where were You for that?"

Bobby stopped in front of his window and looked up into the dark night.

"If You are good," he shouted at the top of his lungs, "and if You really do care about me, well then, tell me, where were You when Willie drowned?

"He was just a boy! Why couldn't You have let him live? Couldn't You have saved him?" Bobby raised his arms and shrugged his shoulders. "Huh? Why won't You answer me? Why couldn't You have saved him?"

Bobby dropped his arms back down and lowered his voice. "Why couldn't You have saved me?"

23

ON THE SAME SIDE

As Bobby walked into the hotel gym, he subconsciously lifted the collar of his sweatshirt and bit down on it. It was an old habit he had developed when training for wrestling. Anytime he was upset or his adrenaline was pumping, he would stick his shirt or some piece of cloth into his mouth and bite down, gritting his teeth and locking his jaw so tight that he almost always bit holes straight through the fabric. He grabbed a couple of weights and walked over to the treadmill.

That morning he had woken up to find himself lying face down on his hotel room floor at the foot of his bed. He had spent the entire night and well into the morning fighting to find some answers, but had found nothing. He had come before God, laid out all of his angers and pain, and met complete silence. After several hours of fighting, he had eventually just given up and passed out—physically, mentally, and emotionally exhausted.

Bobby lifted the weights and started to curl them as he ran on the treadmill's highest possible incline. Working out was always therapeutic for him. It was a way for him to release his aggression, to get his blood flowing, and to keep his mind off of everything else. But at this moment, it didn't do him an ounce of good. Even though he wanted to give his mind and his emotions a break, nothing could distract him from his quest to find resolution.

I need an answer. I need to know what He is like. Bobby glanced around the gym; even though he knew it was empty, he double-checked just to make sure.

"You weren't there for me when I needed You," Bobby panted. He needed to hear his own voice. He needed to make his thoughts clear instead of letting them bounce around uncontrollably in his head.

"Throughout my entire life I've been on my own. I've had to take care of myself, had to protect myself, and had to provide for myself." Bobby paused the treadmill and set down the weights.

"And you know what? I've made it out okay." He immediately thought back to his wall of trophies. In all manners of social standards he had excelled over his CMSU years: that much was undeniable. "I got my act together, figured some things out, and look at me now! I'm doing great." Although they were statements, each sentence hung in the air like a question. *Do I really have my act together? Am I really doing great?*

"Maybe You haven't been there because I didn't need Your help," Bobby rationalized. "Maybe that's the lesson to be learned. You help those who help themselves. Maybe, I'm supposed to be able to handle life all on my own."

The sound of someone sliding their key card through the door caused him to snap out of his one-way conversation with God. Bobby turned around and nodded at the young man who walked into the room and then he grabbed the dumbbells and resumed his workout.

——— - - ———

The next morning, sitting alone in a corner table of the hotel's crowded breakfast area, Bobby drank his third cup of coffee, trying desperately to pull himself out of the fog he was in. After working out the previous afternoon, he had returned back to his room and had again spent the entire night trying to wrestle out an answer to the nature of God. And yet again, he had come away with more questions than answers.

After his initial conversation with George, when he had first set out to ask all of these questions, Bobby had thought the process was going to be beneficial. Even if nothing happened, he would have at least gotten all of his pains and fears out on to the table to address them. So many of his wounds had been hidden deep inside and he figured it could only be a good thing to get them out in the open.

Boy was I wrong, he thought while refilling yet another cup of coffee. He had brought up all these pains and it had done nothing but pour salt in the wound. He shook his head and sighed. *I should've never done any of this.* His thoughts drifted to Bernie. *Maybe he had the right idea all along. Maybe I shouldn't have tried to take any of this God stuff seriously.*

"Excuse me, young man, do you think I could join you?" A woman Bobby guessed to be in her early forties approached his table.

"Oh, yeah, absolutely," Bobby said, shoving his empty cups off to the side so that she had room to put her plate down.

The women introduced herself to Bobby as Hannah and struck up a conversation. It was a welcome distraction for Bobby to have someone to talk to, and her kind and joyful spirit soothed Bobby's aching soul. After a few minutes of conversation, Bobby was taken aback by how much Hannah reminded him of his own mother. Like his mother, Hannah seemed to have a witty remark for everything, an infectious smile, and an ability to light up the whole room with her laugh.

For all the difficult memories he had from his mother's pain, there were easily just as many beautiful memories. But as Hannah talked, her words and mannerisms tore down Bobby's bitterness, and all the good memories and sentiments came flooding back.

After a little while, Hannah stood up and thanked Bobby for sharing his table. But before leaving she turned back around and looked Bobby in the eyes.

"You are going to be okay," she said with a reassuring smile, and then she turned and walked away.

Bobby was taken aback by her statement. He had not told her anything about his struggles over the last few days. But then again, Bobby had begun to develop a habit of wearing his emotions on his sleeve. Maybe she had sensed the turmoil Bobby was going through; perhaps that is why she had sat down in the first place.

Bobby grabbed one more cup of coffee and then walked back to his room and sat down on his bed. His brief interaction with Hannah was still reverberating inside of him. The interaction had provoked feelings of joy and nostalgia, but it had also provoked a feeling of great loss. He had forgotten what it was like to be a part of a family, to love and be loved unconditionally. Ever since he had left his house, he had been on his own, and never had he truly realized how lost that had made him feel.

I don't want to be alone anymore. The thought struck him with a profound weight.

He thought back on the last words his father had said about his mom before Bobby walked out the door: "I promised to love her all of her life when I married her, and I plan on keeping that promise. Whether she ever gets better or not, I will never stop loving her."

Bobby thought about his response: "Dad, I just don't have that kind of love."

That was I told him. 'Dad I just don't have that kind of love.' Bobby began to weep. *Even in the midst of her pain, there was still so much to love. Why couldn't I have seen it?*

Bobby slowly knelt back down by the bed. He had wrestled with the idea that maybe he didn't even need God, that he could handle everything on his own. *But maybe I don't want to be on my own.*

"I don't want to be alone, I..." Bobby searched for the right words to say but he couldn't find them. So, instead, he lowered his face into his hands and didn't say a single thing, didn't ask another question, and didn't make an accusation—he just kept quiet and listened. He thought about his life, his successes, and his failures. They just all seemed so pointless. All of his life he had tried to hide himself from his feelings of being lost and alone. He had tried to wrestle away his fears. He had tried to keep himself so busy he couldn't think about his pain. He had tried so hard to excel in every area of life so that he could be proud of himself. But he had never learned how to love.

After several minutes, Bobby found his voice.

"If you really are a God who sees me and who cares about me—well, then, I need You." His words were full of a genuine desperation. "I'm a simple child, and I need Your help."

What happened next was the single most incredible and life-changing moment Bobby Hartley had ever experienced. He suddenly realized that the presence of God was there with him in the room.

He felt the room light up, and an intense heat began to emanate from behind him, as if the entire back wall of his hotel room had caught on fire. Immediately, he knew that the One he had been searching for was standing there behind him, more real than life itself. He kept his eyes closed and his head down, frozen in an awesome fear. In an instant, all of Bobby's anger and pain were gone—as though a physical burden had been lifted from his shoulders. The weight of despair disappeared in the midst of such a holy and powerful presence. The simple nearness of the Spirit of God was enough to answer all of Bobby's questions, but then He spoke:

"Every demon from hell has been loosed against you, because they know who you are." The voice of God spoke softly to Bobby, each word hitting Bobby like a surge of electricity. More than just hearing the voice out loud, he could feel it coursing through him. "Can we get on the same side?"

Each moment that the Lord spoke exponentially expanded Bobby's world as waves of love and compassion washed through to his very core.

"You have asked Me where I was." The voice grew stronger and echoed like thunder across the room. "Bobby, where were you? I've tried to put you under the umbrella of My love and you've stepped out and got hurt. And then you have turned around and blamed Me," the voice said sternly, yet with a compassionate sense of clarity.

"I have always been there for you, Bobby. Don't you remember when I was there for you in the cubby hole?"

Then, as if he were dreaming, Bobby suddenly saw the past in greater detail than memory could allow. He saw himself, a young lost boy tucked in a corner between the two brick walls, scribbling poems inside of his green journal.

"Don't you remember how you would pretend how I was good? How you would pretend that I was there beside you?" The voice continued, "Bobby, won't you realize, you were never pretending!"

The scene changed to Mike O'Hara's driveway as Bobby helped his friend up after he had taken a beating on Bobby's behalf. Mike's words hung in the air: "You're my best friend. Of course I would fight for you."

"Bobby that was Me," the Lord said. "Don't you know I will always fight for you?"

Bobby saw himself on the I-71 railing again, hundreds of feet above the ground. Except this time, Bobby could see the presence of two angels standing on either side of him, steadying his foolish steps.

"I have always loved you," the voice of the Lord explained. Bobby saw himself lying beneath the bushes of Aunt May's house as she sat on her porch swing proclaiming prayers of faith and love over Bobby's life. "And through the voices of those who have surrounded you, I have echoed this love."

There was a glimpse of Bobby pounding on the doors of the hotel elevator, William standing there behind him. William's words echoed in Bobby's heart. *"Today I lost Little Willie. Bobby, I don't want to lose you, too."*

"Even when you were at your lowest, I never, ever, left your side."

The images flashed by, revealing hundreds of moments when the Lord was there right alongside of him: when Joe the swim instructor spoke wisdom to Bobby, when Bobby woke up in the middle of the night suddenly aware that he needed to leave his house, when he flipped the delivery truck and the Lord sat next to him on the side of the road comforting him. The moments rolled on and on, and then, finally, he saw himself back at the table during his family's Thanksgiving dinner. Bobby was met with the memory of his father looking into his eyes.

"I'm proud of you, son." The words of his father were more alive than they had ever been. "I know you. You are going to pin your problems to the mat. You going to be quite a man someday, and you are going to touch a lot of lives."

While the other pictures had flashed by, this one slowed. The moment washed over Bobby for what seemed like forever. Consumed with his father's love, Bobby began to weep.

"I have always been there for you, Bobby, and I always will be. I gave your father a glimpse of the plan I have for your life."

Bobby was then given a final image, except this time, it wasn't a memory. It was a picture of his future, and it was something more beautiful than Bobby could've ever imagined.

"You *are* going to be quite a man someday, and you *are* going to touch a lot of lives."

And for the first time, Bobby fully believed those familiar words.

Then, as quickly as he had been taken away, Bobby found himself back in his hotel room. He began to feel the weight of the presence lighten as the Lord spoke these final words.

"There will be those that will tell you that this is not true, that this is not the story of your life. Don't believe them."

24

COMING HOME

Bobby walked back to his car that was parked just down the road from his parents' house. He had knocked on his parents' door, but no one responded. *They must not be home. I'll come back later,* he thought, a little bit relieved.

In the passenger seat of the car, a pile of poorly wrapped gifts sat stacked on top of one another—trinkets he had picked up at convenience stores on his drive back into Kansas City from CMSU. He had been mostly removed from his family's lives for the past seven years, and now he was coming back bearing gifts of key chains, gas cards, and a plastic sixty-four ounce Big Gulp cup.

It had been one week since his encounter with God in the Chicago hotel room and everything had changed. Immediately after the encounter, he had dedicated his life to following Christ.

He was not really sure what that meant or what it would like, but whatever it took, Bobby was completely and wholeheartedly invested in his relationship with the Lord.

"I'm putting my whole life in a bag and handing it over to You," Bobby had promised after his encounter. His whole life: pains and victories of the past, worries and dreams for the future, they were all in God's hands now.

Bobby sat down inside of his car and put the keys into the ignition. *What am I going to say when I do see them?* How was he was supposed to explain all of this to his family? He hadn't really had much interaction with them in years, and now he was just showing up at their house with this crazy story. Would they even believe him? *Hey Mom and Dad, sorry I've been gone for so long, but guess what? I found Jesus, and now I want us to be a family again.* Bobby sighed. This wasn't going to be an easy conversation.

He turned the engine on, but just before he was about to pull away, a car rolled up and parked in his parents' driveway. Bobby stopped and watched as his father got out of the car and shuffled his way to the trunk. John's hair had begun to grey and his steps had slowed. As he pulled a couple of bags of groceries out of his trunk, he winced in pain from the strain it put on his back.

One of the most profound revelations Bobby had during his experience in the Chicago hotel rooms came from realization of how much he needed help. He had always believed that it was an "every man for himself" kind of world, and so he had built his life around fighting his battles on his own. But now everything was changing.

It was a long time coming, but he was finally realizing how much he needed his family. He couldn't keep on fighting life's battles alone. And as Bobby watched his father, he began to realize that maybe his family needed him, too. He knew he couldn't make up for leaving them in the first place, but suddenly it wasn't about making up for the mistakes of the past. It was about what he could do now.

He got out of his car and headed toward his father.

When he gave his life to the Lord, he had no idea where his journey would lead him. But at least he knew the first step: learning how to love his family.

25

CLEANING THEATERS WITH HITLER'S DESCENDANT

"Your trash is our cash! Your filth, our future!"

This was the motto of Hartley's Executive Cleaners, a company Bob created a few years after I was born. Cleaning carpets was a Bob Hartley specialty, and when I was fourteen years old, he convinced me to join him for a road trip down to clean some theater carpets in Arizona.

"Come on, Bud! It will be a blast!" Dad said, with far more excitement then I thought was normal for a grown man.

"Yeah, I don't know, Dad." I was not a huge fan of road trips or cleaning theaters or manual labor in general for that matter.

"Oh, come on, Slick. You'll have fun. A couple of men out on the road; you need a little bit more manliness in your life," Dad said, as he looked at the scrawny 5′-2″ kid standing before him.

We both sighed involuntarily, each of us secretly wishing there could've been another boy in the family. It would've been so much easier if I wasn't the solitary embodiment of the Bob Hartley legacy. Come on, that's at least a two-man job.

"Okay, I'll schedule the trip from a Monday to a Thursday," he said, switching tactics. "I'll get you out of almost a whole week of school."

"Now you're speaking my language, Pops," I said, as we gave each other a high five and began to conspire on how we could swing it by Mom.

A few weeks later, I was climbing into the Hartley's Executive Cleaners extractor van with my dad. It had become a pretty exciting opportunity once I had committed to it. Skipping school to go on a road trip with my dad—no homework, no distractions, just two men on the open road, eating whatever they wanted, with no maternal influence telling them they couldn't.

However, as I climbed into the van I became aware of some inconveniences I had not yet considered. I was sitting in what was essentially a gutted delivery van with a large extractor machine in the back that was powered by the vehicle's engine. The process of cleaning carpets with the van was fairly simple: you put hot water and some cleaning chemicals on the carpet, buff the carpet to knock loose all the dirt, and then use a wand with a long hose connected to the extractor in the van to suck up all the water. The results were incredible; an old, stained carpet could look like new.

The only problem was that all of that dirty hot water was sucked into a large tank inside the van, which gave it a permanent and rather unpleasant smell. "Unpleasant" is an understatement.

"Unbearable" is much more accurate. After about ten minutes of marinating in the stench of the vehicle, any measure of excitement I had once possessed completely disappeared.

"So, you might want to roll down the window, because the air conditioner is broken and this thing really heats up after driving for a bit," Dad announced casually, while chewing on some beef jerky he had stashed for the trip. His stash also included trail mix and Twinkies—enough, he figured, to sustain us all the way to Arizona without having to waste time eating at restaurants.

I tried to roll down the window but nothing happened.

"Oh, yeah, I forgot," Dad said through a mouthful of jerky, "that window is broken."

I began to panic; I felt trapped inside a traveling sauna with the distinct smell of cleaning chemicals, dirty buffer pads, and raunchy theater carpet juice. The smell became so overpowering that you could taste it as much as smell it. And now we couldn't even open the windows to get a breath of fresh air.

We stopped at a gas station a few hours into the trip. While Dad went inside to use the restroom, I seriously contemplated making a break for the highway and hitchhiking back to Kansas City. On one hand, I was only fourteen, and my mom had taught me that hitchhiking was dangerous. On the other hand, remaining in that vehicle for another fourteen hours was practically suicidal. I tightened my shoelaces and stepped outside.

Just as I was about to make a mad dash for the road, Dad came bounding out of the gas station. He tossed me an ice cream sandwich and took a swig of a sixty-four-ounce cup of his favorite soda concoction: equal parts Diet Dr. Pepper, Diet Coke, and raspberry ice tea, with just a dash of hot coffee and maybe a squirt of Tabasco sauce.

"This is an adventure, Buddy!" Dad pronounced with a beaming smile. It was incredible how much he was enjoying all of this.

I have always operated under the assumption that my father has a disease. I'm sure there is a scientific word for it, but I just call it *crazy*. And, apparently, it's either contagious or hereditary, because the light in his eyes and the hop in his step sparked an excitement in me as well. I caught the crazy.

I jumped back in the car, and, as I chomped down on my ice cream sandwich and grabbed a handful of trail mix, the smell suddenly wasn't so overwhelming. This was fun; this was dangerous; this was an adventure!

That night, we arrived at our hotel around ten o'clock. The theater was closing at midnight and Dad was planning on working from closing time until it opened again at ten the next morning. However, he was a bit concerned. The process was really a three-man job and he began to wonder whether we would be able to finish before the theater opened the next day. He called a local temp agency and arranged for a worker to help us clean the theater.

I hadn't yet told my dad, but I was starting to feel a little sick. The eleven ice cream sandwiches and fifteen Twinkies weren't sitting particularly well with me. I didn't want to tell him I was feeling sick because he always handled sickness in the most unusual way: he would play a tough psychological game with you, telling you there is no way you are sick and you better not think about it because it is merely a mind game. Unfortunately, I felt so ill, I just had to tell him.

"Dad, I don't feel good," I said, as we were walking to the van.

"Nope, you feel fine!" he responded, convincingly.

"No, I think I'm sick," I said, slightly confused about why he knew more about my own body than I did.

"No, you're a healthy kid. Don't think about it and you'll be fine."

You see, my dad is a man of extremes. Whenever I am actually indisputably sick or in pain, I only need say "I'm running a fever" or "There is an excess amount of blood" or "I'm throwing up," and he suddenly turns into the world's most concerned medical expert.

And sure enough, just before we stepped into the van, when I turned and began throwing up all over the parking lot Dad was immediately all concern.

"Oh, no, Jed!" he exclaimed. "I'll get you help! We can get some medicine! I saw a Walgreens back there. Let me feel your head. Oh, it's hot! You should lie down. I'll get you some ice. Should I elevate your feet? I think there is a hospital nearby. I will call; we can take you to the emergency room—" He continued like this for quite some time.

Finally, I stopped throwing up and reassured my dad that I did not in fact need emergency surgery.

"I think I just ate something bad, Dad. I'm fine, we can go."

After some convincing, we got into the van and headed to the theater. My dad made me a deal that I could sit in one of the movies that was just finishing up, drink some water, and, after thirty minutes or so, if I was still feeling ill, he would take me home. But hey, I'm a Hartley, and a simple Twinkie and ice cream sandwich overdose cannot hold me down. I made a speedy recovery and headed out to help him as he started to set up the van.

A few minutes after midnight, a tall, skinny, African American man with long dreadlocks and bright blue eyes stepped out of a taxi and introduced himself to us as Schmidt. Schmidt was the temporary worker we had hired and he was ready to help. He had a firm handshake and a bright smile, and I remember that, at first, I really liked him. Then he started talking.

Moments after meeting us, he announced that he was a proud descendant of Adolph Hitler. It's not like he worked it into the conversation, either. It went more like: "Hey, which cleaning chemical should I use? Oh, and by the way, I am a descendent of Adolf Hitler!"

"But, you're black," I said.

He responded by grabbing my shoulders and pressing his face close to mine.

"Look me in the eyes," Schmidt said.

"Okay," I responded.

"See these blue eyes? These are the eyes of Hitler."

"Okay."

I thought that was kind of creepy.

My mom had been worried about us being out late at night because there was a serial killer at large in Arizona. For real. It had been all over the news and she made me promise that I would stay inside the theater while we were working. I wondered perhaps if she would make an exception because I was fairly confident Dad had, in fact, hired that same serial killer, and he was now in the theater with us.

Dad was at a loss. I could see it on his face. He wore the same perplexed, confused, and frightened look he always displayed when one of my sisters would suddenly burst into tears. His concern concerned me, because, other than when he is at the mercy of the women in our household, it was not often that Dad visibly showed fear. In fact, beyond his inexplicably acute phobia of caves and ballpoint pens, I never really knew my dad to be afraid of anything.

For a few moments, we all continued to work in silence, but silence never lasts long when in the presence of Bob Hartley.

"You are so good! You're abundantly available in our time of need. A friend who sticks closer than a brother," Dad began to pray aloud, his booming, gravelly voice cutting the silence and echoing through the large auditorium.

It startled Schmidt, but not me; I was used to it. When my dad became a Christian, he quickly became a firm believer in the power of audible prayer. Just weeks after he was saved, he would go to a bar, stand on a table, and begin to shout his prayers aloud. Not your conventional prayers, either; he used his prayers to tell God who He was. Just as a person might profess their love to their spouse, Dad would profess his love to God, telling Him the hundreds of different reasons He is wonderful.

Like in the movies, when the love-struck boy runs through the streets, yelling at the top of his lungs about his incomparable affection, it is always quite a spectacle. Of course, in the movies, you think it's cute and everyone claps and cheers because they understand and appreciate the boy's conviction. No one, however, understands my dad when he spontaneously starts praising the Lord in public.

Few things are as embarrassing as when your dad stands up at your high school football game and starts shouting love for the Deity like a mad man. Or when you're walking down the street in crowded downtown New York City and you suddenly hear your father screaming at the top of his lungs, "Oh Lord! You are so good! Jesus, You saved all these people; I just want them to know You! I want them to see Your beautiful face!"

That one happened to me just a couple of months ago.

Also recently, while traveling on a flight from Mexico, Dad spent the last half of the trip proclaiming the goodness of God. Everyone within eleven rows heard him pray for two hours straight.

I have often told him how embarrassing this is for anyone around him. In response, he has, quite inaccurately, come to the conclusion that I am "a cool dude" who likes to "fly under the radar." Sometimes I wonder if he realizes just how odd and unconventional he can be. I'm not really an under-the-radar kind of guy. In fact, I'm quite the extrovert, myself. But I usually stop short of actually making a spectacle.

A lot of people are put off by being somewhat forcibly subjected to Dad's public proclamation of his faith, but on the other hand, I can't tell you how many individuals have been transformed because of it.

And Schmidt was one of those individuals.

At first, Schmidt just stared at Dad, confused. He even turned to me and whispered, "Is this dude crazy? Who the [word that should never be spoken to a fourteen-year-old] is this guy talking to?"

I understood Schmidt's confusion, but then again, Mr. "look-me-in-my-Hitler-eyes" probably didn't have the credentials to be handing out crazy cards.

So, there I was, stuck between odd and odder, just watching events unfold. After about two hours, Schmidt started to nod his head every once in a while, confirming that he was not only listening to Dad's prayers, but also agreeing with them. After about four hours, he would chime in with an occasional "Amen!" or "Hallelujah, brother!" It was fascinating to watch.

We worked for ten straight hours and not once did Dad stop praying. When we finished, Schmidt thanked him and asked if we wouldn't mind giving him a ride home. I still thought he could be a serial killer so I wasn't too excited about that, but, of course, Dad said yes. On the way, Schmidt broke down in tears and spent the entire ride explaining how he was a backsliding believer who wanted desperately to get his life back together.

I wondered if backsliding for him meant murdering people. I was still pretty fixated on the whole serial killer possibility. Fortunately, Dad wasn't. Before Schmidt got out of the van, Dad prayed with him that he would be able to reconnect with his heavenly Father and get his life on track. Schmidt thanked Dad and hugged him as if they had been best friends since childhood. He walked into his house, I truly believe, a transformed man with far more hope and faith than the one we had met a few hours earlier.

It was, altogether, one of the most eventful and exhausting nights of my life, and as Schmidt stepped in his house and my dad turned the van around to head toward the hotel, I relaxed, leaned my head back, and fell asleep.

I awoke no less than five minutes later to a loud, rhythmic, thudding noise. Startled, I looked outside to see our van drifting into a long line of construction cones blocking off the right lane of the highway.

WHACK! WHACK! WHACK!

Cone after cone went flying as our car played Pac-Man on the construction safety line. I looked over at my dad. Hands on the wheel and foot on the gas, Dad was fast asleep.

I yelled, "Dad!" He awoke with a start, jerking us back into the left lane, almost overcorrecting and sending us careening into the highway median.

"Oh sorry, sorry," Dad sputtered, as he shook his head in an attempt to revive himself.

"You almost killed us!" I exclaimed.

"No, it's okay. I had one eye open," he replied.

"I'm pretty sure you were snoring," I retorted, knowing that he was absolutely fast asleep.

"No, just breathing heavy. It's okay. I'm awake. You can go back to sleep," he said convincingly.

I nodded and tried my best to slow my breathing. Between this and Schmidt the possible serial killer, my nerves had just about reached their limit for a single day.

"Okay, well, you should pull over if you're too tired," I said.

"No, no, I'm fine. We're only ten minutes away."

Hesitantly, I rested my head back and shut my eyes again. Just seconds later....

WHACK! WHACK! WHACK!

My eyes shot open just in time to see an orange cone slide up over our windshield and flip wildly through the air.

"Dad!" I yelled again. Again, he woke up with a start, almost careening into the median.

"What are you doing? Pull over!"

"I just had the best dream," Dad said.

There are a few sentences you never, ever want to hear from the driver of a vehicle. "I just had the best dream" is certainly one of them.

"Can you please pull over?" I implored, but Dad wasn't having it.

"Nah, we can make it home."

For some reason, the distinct possibility of crashing and dying was not something too frightening to my father, for not only did he continue driving, but he continued to fall asleep while driving. I, of course, now wide awake, sat and watched his eyes vigilantly. Any time he started to nod off, I would slap his arm. After about eight minutes, and at least eleven slaps, we finally made it to the hotel safely.

"You know, you probably would be dead right now if I hadn't been in the van to wake you up!" I said as we walked to our hotel room.

"I used to fall asleep at the wheel all the time while driving a delivery van when I was in college," Dad replied casually.

Wait, what? Was he being for real? This was like a regular thing for him?

"I'm a good driver in my sleep," he continued.

I didn't even know how to process what he was saying to me…a good driver in his sleep?

"You never wrecked?" I asked.

"Yeah, I guess I did. One time, I flipped the van a few times and had to smash the window and crawl out, because I thought it was about to catch on fire." He said this with such nonchalance, you would've thought he was talking about tomorrow's weather forecast.

I honestly had no idea if he was making this story up or not. Normally I would've required further proof before believing it. But then again, he had just driven about fourteen miles while half asleep. What kind of history did he have where almost dying was not enough of an event to keep him awake?

As I crawled into bed that night (well, actually that *day*, considering that it was now almost eleven in the morning), I pondered the events of the past twenty four hours.

I had been nearly asphyxiated by driving in our extractor van, also known as the traveling sauna of deathly stench. I got food poisoning, made friends with Hitler's kid, and nearly crashed and died at the hands of a self-proclaimed professional narcoleptic vehicle operator.

Yep, just a normal day living with Bob Hartley.

—— - - ——

I have looked back upon our experience with Schmidt many times as I've grown older. In one sense it embodied everything I couldn't understand about my dad's ministry. Both my dad and I are extroverts and verbal processors, yet our interactions with those around us couldn't be more different. I enjoy being around people, hearing their stories, and viewing their lives, but rarely do I like to get too involved in the shaping of someone's life. I respect boundaries and seldom force myself into someone's comfort zone unless invited. I have many acquaintances, but only a few close friends at a time.

My dad, however, becomes best friends with just about everyone he meets. He has no distinction between public and private; he will tell his entire life story, including many of his most painful and personal moments, to someone he just met on the subway. And he expects the same from them. He always assumes these complete strangers will suddenly divulge their most intimate secrets to him, almost instantaneously, and, oddly enough, they often do.

Imagine for a moment that people are like paintings in a museum. I would prefer to go into the museum with a camera and a notepad, analyzing and appreciating the beauty of each painting. Bob Hartley goes in with a paintbrush and a can of paint, running around and slapping improvements upon every canvas he sees.

"Oh, hey, this lady looks sad; let me paint a smile on her." He would bounce around, "improving" all the paintings within the museum until he is eventually thrown out by security.

My instinct stands aloof in the corner of the gallery, silently cheering on the security guards.

"Respect people; give them space," I would often correct my dad.

Schmidt honestly was a bit put off by Dad's prayers, especially since Dad gave him absolutely no option but to listen to them for several hours straight. But by the end of our time together, Schmidt was asking Dad how he could get his life together. Dad's prayers changed his life.

Dad's methods are unconventional. You could even argue that they are intrusive. Yet they made, and continue to make, an impact.

26

AN ODD FAMILY

One morning in high school, I heard a voice breaking through my dreams.

"Buddy, you slept in! You're gonna be late for school!"

I pried my eyes open as my dad shook me out of a deep slumber. I was halfway through my junior year in high school and had already nearly exhausted my year's allowance of tardy arrivals to class. I leapt out of my bed and quickly embraced my dad.

"Oh, no! Thanks for waking me up!" I grabbed some clothes and headed towards the shower.

"Hey, no problem," Dad said, with a smile.

I flipped on the shower and hopped in without waiting for the water to warm up. It was the dead of winter in Kansas City and

I couldn't help but let out a yelp when I was hit with the water which, in the words of Andre 3000, was "cooler than being cool."

Accomplishing the dual benefit of not being late and not getting hypothermia, I showered at lightning speed, ran downstairs, and poured myself a bowl of cereal. While munching on my sizable bowl of Honey Bunches of Oats, I noted that it was still dark outside. But I didn't give it much thought—it was still mid-January and the sun normally didn't show itself until just before school started.

My thoughts turned to my homework assignments. Had I finished everything? Was there a test today? My brain normally took a while to warm up, especially in the winter, but I was having an abnormal amount of difficulty remembering what I had scheduled for the day.

I finished my bowl of cereal and headed back to my room to grab my keys and backpack. As I walked back up the stairs, I began to notice a couple of anomalies. Where was my mom? She was always up before me. For that matter, where were the dogs? They never, ever, slept past six in the morning. What time was it?

I poked my head into my parents' room and saw my mom lying in her bed fast asleep. Our dog, Winston, who slept on the floor of my parents' room, slowly picked up his head and lazily looked at me, as if to say, "Why the heck are you up at this hour?" I glanced at my mom's clock; it read 3:16 A.M. I pulled my phone out of my pocket for verification. Sure enough, it was the middle of the night, and on top of that, it was Saturday. I processed this information for several moments. Then, finally, it clicked.

About two weeks ago, I had moved from my room in the basement to our family's guest room. The room was bigger, and I found the guest room bed to be considerably more comfortable. For years, however, my dad, who sometimes has trouble sleeping through the night, had developed a habit of getting up in the middle of the night and reading. He couldn't turn on the light in his room because of both my mom and Winston, so he would always head to the guest room to read (he also found the guest room bed to be considerably more comfortable). Earlier that morning, when my dad had gotten up and noticed that I was now occupying his favorite late-night reading spot, he decided to perform an ouster.

I walked back down the hallway toward my bedroom and slowly opened the door. Snuggled beneath the covers of my bed, my dad slowly lowered a book he had in front of his face, revealing a wry smile. He looked at me and smugly giggled.

"You are a very unusual man," I said.

He slapped the bed and smiled. "Come on, you can come cuddle with your daddy."

I slept downstairs.

—— – – ——

After twenty-two years, I have concluded two major things concerning my father:

Number one: I sure hope I grow up to be like my mother.

Number two: I could not have asked for a better dad.

—— – – ——

At some point in our lives, I believe we all question, at least briefly, why we were placed in our family—like when your own father convinces you you're late for school only so he can steal your bed as you rush downstairs in a panic. It's just a little hard during those times not to wonder why you couldn't have been placed in a more normal family.

While growing up, I was frequently asked, "So who did you get your blonde curly hair from?"

It was a valid question: my parents both have straight dark hair, my grandparents all had straight hair, and heck, besides one of my uncles, nobody in my extended family even had curly hair. I was often befuddled by the question myself. "Everyone else has straight dark hair, so why am I the anomaly?" I have finally concluded that the answer is one of two very distinct possibilities: either (a) who knows who I got it from, it's a recessive gene, sometimes things like this happen, or (b) I am not my parents' offspring, and everything I have ever known is a lie.

I prefer the former, but the latter is certainly a compelling thought that I have yet to completely dismiss. Maybe I was adopted, and my parents just didn't have the heart to tell me. Or perhaps they themselves didn't know. Maybe I was accidentally switched in the hospital nursery.

Not that I never really felt out of place in my family; I just felt oddly confused by the assortment of personalities that had been injected into it. I mean, if God is an omniscient Being, wouldn't He have known better than to cram all of these personalities together into one family? It's like throwing Mentos in a bottle of Diet Coke, shaking it up, and not expecting the ensuing explosion. So, rather than question God's omniscience, I often assume the mix-up was actually just the fault of some absentminded maternity nurse.

Every time my dad would be, well, himself, shouting prayers in the streets or driving to Arizona to clean a carpet, I would ponder if I had a tall, skinny and completely normal biological father with blonde curly hair out there in the world somewhere. I felt huge compassion for my normal biological father, as now he was taking care of an unruly, muscle-bound troublemaker who was actually the biological son of Bob Hartley.

But then one day, while eating dinner with my family, my little sister Taylor said something that helped change my perception of my family. We were discussing the convoluted mixture of odd thinkers we had in our family. And in the middle, Taylor, who was no more than thirteen at the time, decided to derail the conversation.

"You know, when I look at all of you guys, I don't know if this is quite the assortment of individuals I would have chosen for family members."

As she paused, we all stopped eating and looked at her with raised eyebrows. My dad and I glanced at each other and then back at her wearing an identical expression that said, "Yeah, well, we probably wouldn't have chosen you either, punk." After all, this was the girl who had spent the entire last year speaking in a thick Russian accent for no decipherable reason beyond the fact that she considered it funny. I could tell Dad was about to respond with some sort of snarky comment when Taylor quickly finished her thought.

"But I'm sure glad it happened this way."

As a thirteen-year-old, she had stumbled upon something I am just now beginning to understand myself. I couldn't tell you exactly why I was put in the family I am in, why we all butt heads and life philosophies, or why my dad and I have zero points of agreement besides the Kansas City Chiefs. But I sure as heck am glad it turned out this way.

27

SO NOW WHAT?

There are like no books on how to be a better son. Seriously, I looked it up. On Amazon.com I found pages and pages of books on how to be a better parent—"scream-free" approaches, "nurture" approaches, even one written by a "child whisperer." But none flipped the perspective over to my side, the kid's side; nobody wrote for an adult who wants to be better at this son thing. Which I think is kind of a bummer, because I could really use a book like that right now.

Growing up, my father was my training wheels. He was there to guide me, direct me, keep me in line, and keep from hurting myself. He was also much more than this: he was my counselor, my coach, my favorite storyteller, and my friend. And there were definitely a few times when he would get me into trouble rather than keeping me from it. But at the end of the day, he knew his role was to train me up as a child in the way that I should go.

But now the time has come where I'm to set those training wheels aside. I am no longer a kid and, although I most certainly could use them every now and again, it would be better for me to fall and scrape myself a few times than to become too reliant on their stability. Which puts my Dad and me at an odd place. Our roles in each other's lives are changing, and neither one of us knows exactly how to handle it. He can't be my training wheels, but at the same time it's incredibly difficult to ride alongside each other, because I often brake to admire the view while he cycles faster and faster to get the most extreme workout possible.

But as hard as the transition has been, it's also been extremely beneficial, because I've had the opportunity to look at him from a different vantage point: not just as Bob Hartley my father but, more importantly, as Bob Hartley the man. And in doing so, my respect has only grown.

I told you the story of my dad as a kid trying to rebuild the seawall my grandfather had destroyed. It's one of my favorite stories because it gives a fantastic picture of how we are to relate to our heavenly Father. From a practical standpoint, little Bobby trying to put together the seawall was an exercise in futility and a total waste of energy. But to my grandfather, it was an inestimably precious demonstration of love. And it is the same way with God. Value does not come from that which we accomplish but from how we love our Father. And for as long as I can remember, my Dad has been constantly throwing himself into that water desperately trying to care for the heart of his heavenly Father.

This desire has led Bob Hartley to impact countless lives and build marvelous things, but his ambition has also led him to throw himself into waters way over his head. Sometimes literally. Let me illustrate. One year, Dad couldn't fly out for a much-anticipated family vacation in California because, just a few days before the trip, he ruptured his ear drum while attempting to do a three-and-a-half-back-flip off of the high dive at our local pool. Because high altitudes would have caused him agonizing pain and further damaged his eardrum, Dad decided to drive all the way, with me, meeting the rest of our family at the resort.

However, this meant that the travel time increased from one day to about three, which was simply unacceptable for Bob Hartley. He had been planning for several months how we were going to pray over each family member. He made awards out of paper plates commemorating our spiritual growth during the year and was looking forward to handing them out in a ceremony that would make the Oscars seem short. He had filled at least a dozen spiral notebooks full of the things he believed the Lord wanted to share with us during this vacation time, and now the vacation time was dramatically cut short.

So, greedy for extra time, Dad was determined to drive to California in record time. I vividly remember checking out of our hotel room in Colorado at 4 A.M. after only a few hours of sleep for our second day of travel. As we got in the car, I dosed off immediately while my Dad took the first shift. I woke up hours later and sat up slowly, shielding my eyes from the bright sunlight streaming through the front window. *How come the light is so bright? Shouldn't it be at our backs?* I shot a look toward my dad who was downing his sixth cup of coffee. "Dad, we are heading west, right?" A look of dismay crept upon his face. We weren't. In his ambition and lack of sleep, he had rushed onto the highway and started speeding in the wrong direction.

His ambition has always been, and will always be, one of his most remarkable qualities. But just as it is one of his greatest strengths, it has become one of his greatest weaknesses. His body is becoming less forgiving of his lack of sleep and three-and-a-half-back-flips high dives. Our family is full of adults now and a bit less forgiving of long, drawn-out paper plate ceremonies. And the law, well, has always been rather unforgiving when it comes to speeding down highways. The older I get, the more I realize how unique it is to find a man so dedicated to embracing his calling, loving his family, and seeking after the heart of the Lord. But also, as I get older, I'm finding myself feeling more and more responsible for his journey. He just can't feasibly continue to throw himself into water over his head.

So here we are. It's as if I'm sitting on the edge of the dock, watching as my Dad struggles to rebuild that seawall. And I'm asking myself, *What am I to do? Can I realistically even expect to bring any change to his life?* The man's a runaway freight train fueled by incredible amounts of passion, and he has been on the move since well before I was even born. Do I tell him to stop? Do I try to convince him of a better plan, or at least get him to slow down and take some breaks? Does he even need my help?

In a way, I'm at similar position to my Dad at my age: a guy with a reawakened love for his family, sitting in the car watching his father struggle with the groceries. A guy at a loss for how to enter back into his family's life, but knowing full well that he must. The setting is different but the question is the same: How am I to be a better son?

Both my Dad and I have had the privilege of having fathers who were always there for us. Like my dad, I've learned the high value of that and now have the opportunity to turn around and ask how I can be there for him. It comforts me to know my Dad didn't know exactly how to answer the question of how to be a better son. And what is more comforting is that he is still asking the question—no longer in reference to his earthly father, but in reference to his heavenly Father.

And he, like every one of us who seek to be a better son or daughter to our heavenly Father, doesn't ever know exactly what to do. Whether dragging hoses up through the house, gorging on Twinkies before pulling an all-nighter cleaning theaters, or flying for hours down the highway in the wrong direction, my dad has shown, nay, flaunted, just how prone he is to having the wrong answer. But it wasn't for lack of truly trying. And because of this, I can say, with utmost assurance, that although I will never be a man like him, I hope I can grow up to be a son like him. For Dad has never stopped asking the question of how to be a better son. He has never stopped caring for his Father's heart. And he has never, ever, lost hope.

And that changes lives.

I am not exactly sure how to go about caring for either my earthly or my heavenly Father's heart. But I am taking a page from Dad's book and jumping headfirst into the water to do all I can to help rebuild that seawall. It's alright that I don't know exactly what I am doing. And if I don't actually fix anything, that is okay, too. Maybe I will be able to somehow put that wall back together, or maybe I will accomplish little more than moving a few rocks around. If I pass out from exhaustion, I know my Dad will be there beside me to pull me out—and vice versa. But regardless of what I do or do not accomplish, I will never give up trying, I will never give up caring, and I will never give up hope.

Welcome to Our House!

We Have a Special Gift for You

It is our privilege and pleasure to share in your love of Christian books. We are committed to bringing you authors and books that feed, challenge, and enrich your faith.

To show our appreciation, we invite you to sign up to receive a specially selected **Reader Appreciation Gift**, with our compliments. Just go to the Web address at the bottom of this page.

God bless you as you seek a deeper walk with Him!

WE HAVE A GIFT FOR YOU. VISIT:

whpub.me/nonfictionthx

WHITAKER HOUSE